Cover and interior design: Geoff Munsterman

ISBN: 978-0-938498-12-4 (paperback)
ISBN: 978-0-938498-00-1 (hardcover)

Permissions:

Caroline Rowe: "1. The Fool" from her chapbook *God's Favorite Redhead* (Lucky Bean Press). Alison Pelegrin: "Self-Portrait as 70s Childhood" in *Fine Print*. Andrea Panzeca: "Twins" in the chapbook *Weird... Joe Pesci* (Antenna). Melinda Palacio: "Letter to Time" in *Santa Barbara Literary Journal*. David Havird: "Hurricane Proof" in *Weathering* (Mercer University Press). Ashley Mace Havird: "Gone to Wild" in *Nola Diaspora*. Gina Ferrara: "Ginger Lilies" in *Louisiana Poetry Anthology*. Michael Tod Edgerton: "What Yet Aureate in the Dimming" in *New American Writing 37*. Darrell Bourque: "Hard Rain" in the chapbook *Where I Waited* (Yellow Flag Press). Grace Bauer: "All My Dead Say Grace" published in *Unholy Heart: New and Selected Poems* (University of Nebraska/Backwaters Press). Stacey Balkun: "Benediction" originally published in *Mississippi Review*. Valentine Pierce: "Jimmy's Shoes" published in the book *Jimmy's Shoes* (Portals Press).

EDITED BY
GINA FERRARA & GEOFF MUNSTERMAN

THE
POETRY
BUFFET

AN ANTHOLOGY OF
NEW ORLEANS POETRY

New Orleans Poetry Journal Press

CONTENTS

INTRODUCTION

Beginning In the early 2000s, a formidable group called The Women's Poetry Conspiracy formed in New Orleans to promote readings for female poets. The members of that group were myself, Beverly Rainbolt, Monica Miller, Robin Kemp and Elizabeth Garcia. For a few years, we had readings at different branches of the New Orleans Public Library, with many taking place at The Latter Branch. The head librarian was Missy Abbott (now retired), who pretty much told the group that we could always have readings there, barring anything unforeseen happening. Little did the group know that when Missy made her generous offer to have Latter as a venue for our readings, in August of 2005 hurricane Katrina would create a monumental shift where every person living in or connected to New Orleans would articulate and define time as life before the storm and life after.

Hurricane Katrina scattered the WPC, and to be honest, two years later, when Missy reached out to see if we could resume the series, the city was still hobbling along, slowly resurrecting itself from the aftermath. I expressed uncertainty about resuming, but Missy was adamant. I explained that a few in our group had moved, and those of us who stayed were trying to put our lives back together, so Missy suggested we create a new name. We also talked about how it would be crucial to have readings that represented New Orleans. Post Katrina it was apparent that the readings would better serve the city if they were not just limited to one gender. It was Missy who came up with the idea of naming the series The Poetry Buffet. I remember joking with her and saying that it sounded much better than The Poetry Smorgasbord or The Poetry Cafeteria. The name of the series and the series itself has stuck, now in its sixteenth year of featuring/offering poetry the first Saturday of most months at 2:00 pm.

Because of Covid, The Buffet has adapted, sometimes using Zoom and sometimes using The Latter Branch, which has been a superlative home for the series, thanks to Missy's vision and the commitment of the staff past and present, to bring poetry to the city.

The anthology includes one hundred poets who have read at some point during The Buffet's sixteen year tenure. Enjoy.

Gina Ferrara, spring 2023

THE
POETRY BUFFET

Raina Zelinski

Unlikely Farmers

Standing on the field collecting flowers
Ignoring the quadrilateral sugar
experiment like an obtuse horse wearing flies

You are not kicking any balls
Though the children around you glare and jerk
Jumping tallest, smarter, hotter
Hugging acute angles in outdoor certainty

The forecast calls for prisms today
And your puppy body becomes a curled pyramid
A scalene triangle conducting rainbows

Though skirtless,
You actually turn and dance.
I watch your mouth singing in the outfield
Correct and funny
Hugging your observations

The footballers and you
Rainbow farmers
Unlikely light collectors
Like bottles left at sunset in error.

Andy Young

Purple Jellies

upside down
in aquarium light
the jellies' frilly tentacles
caress the wetness
of their existence
translucent veil
covering their inner workings
are they one are they many
do they know they are alive
they don't need to I guess
existing in the simplest of existences
these only-beings
pulsing deep in space
heartbeats on a sonogram
bodiless brains dreaming themselves
in the brine

Audubon Aquarium of the Americas, 2021

Jan Villarubia

La Bretagne

Tell me about your dimpled hands.
Did they make your *coiffe*, shawl and cape?
That hole in your skirt. How did that happen?

Tell me about the butter cake you just nibbled
after the steaming bowl of *Moules Marinières*.

Tell me about your pet goose you named Lorraine.

I want to sit on the floor at your knee,
hear about freezing Breton nights,
how you climb into your *lit-clos*,
close the door against damp draughts,
sleep warm and safe inside.

Tell me about the ancient church
you enter every morning, the small,
crooked-looking one that calms you
with its candles of honeysmoke,
its utter silence.

Please tell me in your mother tongue.
Or have you gone silent since
children pointed and laughed as
signs in school warned,
Forbidden to speak Breton
or spit on floor.

Nikki Ummel

Former Champion of the Uneven Bars

I used to be a gymnast—
used to launch like a torpedo
from the mat,

            "Explosive energy!" Coach Kim would say.

    After practice, Mom

                rinsed my leotard   in the kitchen,
        and left it to dry   outside on the clothesline.
                I watched it
                   shimmer over the chicken coop,
             casting sequined shadows
                    while our hens clucked.

        When Mom chose stocking the pantry
        over feeding my Olympic dreams,
      and said, *throw that shit away*,
                 I hid the leotard in my
                 underwear drawer.

Afterward, mornings came with routine:
hearing the coffee drip,
stiff boots on the kitchen tile,
        I would slide off my mattress,

                onto the hard floor,
                onto my elbows and knees
                and crawl to the door to
      lock my prying parents out,
    so I could   pluck   my old leotard, those sequins still shiny,
             out of crisp cotton,
             to pull over nonexistent hips.

No blooming breasts,
no burgeoning bumps.
At ten, mirrors tell truths.

I peeled off the spandex,
placed it back, and laid hands
on my bare ten-year-old body, a torpedo
ready to launch.

Randolph Thomas

Light in the House

I got a call one night, someone
had seen a light on in the house.
*You need to do something about
it*, they said. I said I would,
but what could I do besides lie
in bed at night, losing sleep.
When I closed my eyes,
I could see the dark basement,
I could see the rooms. Was it
the kitchen light, a light
in one of the bedrooms?
It was the house I'd grown up
in. It was the house my mother
had aged in, where we'd taken
all of her clothes out of
the closets, laid all of it out
on the bed. We'd brought in
a truck, given away her threadbare
clothes and her shabby furniture.
I got up out of the bed, I went
into the bathroom, stood
in the dark in front of the mirror.
It was too far away, I
was too far away, in this dark
room, looking at myself.

Driving with Bread

I was fourteen, and someone had
to raise my father all over again—his brothers and sisters
just didn't understand home. Seven years before,

I was falling asleep in the backseat of his car
without a seatbelt, hearing the second verse

to *The Guitar Man*, the abrupt switch to AM, the gust
from the open window catching smoke and ash.

But those days,
he stumbled from the party, and shoved the keys
into my palm. I hated life behind the steering wheel,
just as I do now,

but I think I did alright. Besides, he was about to snore
in the passenger seat by the time we had reached
the country road on Barataria. Drunk, he didn't care that

the familiar song by Bread was on the radio again,
singing along to the shadow of trees,
scenery that had somehow turned romantic
in the way that only a teen can find romance amid
a home that had suddenly turned strange a year ago.

But I couldn't keep the ignorance;
it braked in the driveway during the final
lines, seeing Mamma on the doorstep with an open mouth.

She shouted as he woke up, but I didn't stay to listen;
besides, there was homework. And life still had school nights.

Shadow Angelina Starkey

Synesthetic

for Geoff Munsterman

When I first saw you,
you were electric alone.
Seated at the bar, head dipped to pages,
a crush of shoulders on a deeply awake spine.
I imagined what it would be to hold your face—
a Louisiana iris amid the muck of that bar
of fetid men and the women they'd break themselves against.
Of serration masquerading as beautiful words,
their tacit bloat cutting and
self-destruction wielded as cultural contribution.

As though by crafting language they could transcend
the sticky sweet rancidity of themselves,
steeped in that distillation more than the alcohol they poured
over their written work
to later set alight, a desperation that maybe
in burning the truths they'd told
they would free themselves from those same truths hold.

Even through their miasma, I could see you—
palpable hunger devoid of intent to steal,
passion you hadn't let turn predatory,
out of place and glistening back the light of a hidden moon.
An overlooked little brother to already lesser men.

Our next encounter
your body thrummed worn velvet over old bone
Cigarette smoke and a hint of cherries.

You absorbed questions with deliberate eyes and a half smile
that wasn't a smile at all
a bending of plump lip
distraction to sudden focus, sharp as nails on the back of our necks.

The intimacy of placing the expressions of my soul into your hands
was the skill I knew you'd have when you'd eventually finger me.
A touch of char in the scent of whisky barrels; oak, vanilla,
and all of the rich bronze complexity of mountains touching the sea.

Our tongues met,
a celestial adagio.
Reaching for one another in the charcoal dark,
no good reason not to,
finally, sublimely when my operatic hips rose to meet yours
lavender melted and swirled into a livid indigo
flowering bruises to later press and command forth a flood.

You have pulled yourself into me,
your trust playing the piano of my body.
I sing for you in minor keys,
a breathless aria of octaves with the pressure of your
rhapsodic love pressed against and deep inside my throat

On top of you I am supported by the strength of your granite will,
crimson passions,
luminously blushed generosity,
and kinetic silken thrust.
The blackened opalescent feathers of my undulation coaxing
the ecstasy in you to awaken,
unfurl, and flourish.
We bathe in the aquamarine of intimacy
crashing against sadness that bleeds into the deepening smoky viridian green
    of hope.
Sincerity washing over us as the sugar sand of Gulf beaches
under a rosy lilac sky edged in gold.

Your well-tongued language spreads and drips along my curves
coalescing with the ephemeral, eternal, ecclesiastic expressions we

create by breathing close to one another.
Our skin sounds like wind through trees
the covenant of hands gripping bark
The synergy of this desire,
the whisper and rustle of an owl's wings.

We are a study in contrast.
Our connection kaleidoscopic,
texturizing each experience with layers of scales fitting
perfectly together into a smoothness that skin can only aspire to.
All the intricacy of flames that travel the hues of burnt ochre,
venous and arterial red,
into a shimmering cerulean violet,
arriving to a phosphorescent glow.

I receive your yes into my mouth where it melts and lingers,
raspberries and dark chocolate.
Sharp and deep, igniting the muscles in my jaw,
relaxing me as wine on my tongue.
Your hushed murmurs are the gentle touch
of fingertips on cotton rag paper with a deckled edge.
Your poetry tastes of browned butter with a touch of honey.

Together we are hammered copper and sea water creating verdi gris
bearing the lustered patina of every ghost and heartbreak
like graceful warriors
shimmering against an ever-growing darkness.

I can detail the explicit texture and resonant percussion of your stained-glass
    heart,
cobalt vivid and ever illuminated
because the stars shine through it.

Sheryl St. Germain

Credo

I believe in hurricanes and their swirling masses of wind and eye, in cypress trees and crawfish, live or red and spicy and having their heads sucked, I believe in my friend Greg and his sloppy fishing boat, I believe in the Atchafalaya and Lake Pontchartrain and the Mississippi and I believe in alligators and warm summer evenings and snowballs with wedding cake flavor. I believe in catfish and crabs, in mosquitoes and the fog of DDT trucks we used to play in, I believe in polluted lakes and the brave fish that thrive there, in weeds and their tough roots that will grow anywhere, I believe in prairies, in sunburns and cold crisp chardonnays, in Ramos gin fizzes and voodoo dolls, in Mardi Gras beads and tarot cards, in Iowa snow, in water hyacinths and fountain pens, in the sound of cicadas and the light of fireflies. I don't believe in levees anymore but I do believe in floods. I believe in drinking many glasses of wine with friends you love until you both start crying, I believe in mint that never knows when to stop growing, and in the rosemary I plant anew each year because it can't make it through winter. Mostly, I believe in being forgiven, in the way that first touch after years of silence is better than almost everything you believe in.

Christopher Shipman

Hunting for Haunted Houses

Finn asks if we can go—*looking for haunteds*, she calls it.
I've had enough coffee to say yes. I've listened
to the right music and the rain has promised to meet me
on the bridge to the past. Really though
it's going to rain. Soon the clouds will begin
the strangeness of folding in half the distance between
memories and ghosts. I don't mention this.
Finn finds her new toy. Grabs her coat. Five minutes
and we're hunting. She enjoys these little drives.
We always take our aging pug. He rides
in the back with her. His tongue hanging out, fat and pink
like a baby eel. Finn likes knowing how to feel.
A *haunted* means a door is left open. It's as simple as
a cracked window. Peeling paint. Sometimes
you can tell a lawn wants a feral fog to snake through it.
Wants you to imagine it happen. Almost always
there's a second story—at least two—obvious attic above.
The usual jaunt through usual neighborhoods,
none seem right. Here, too many cats curled in too many
tulips. There, the absence of cats and tulips.
Then she spots one—she knows. Three-story brick.
Attic window cracked. White lights strung over shutters
since last Christmas. Front door standing
slightly open. Dim inside like a lie you tell yourself
you never told. In the rearview, Finn's eyes
are like fires. She's proud or her find. I can't help feeling
shitty about our little game. We know nothing
about ghosts that do or don't drift through walls hidden
beyond walls we can see. But neither of us
are ready for me to end this—tell her what's made me

stranger. She asks if the haunted has a basement.
Now she tells the dog that we don't have
a basement at home. I don't say every haunted
has a basement, even if it doesn't. We hunt down another.

Martha Serpas

Ozone

Days are a series of curfews.
        An onshore wind   that moves

the deep   palmetto rales

on narrow paths   through wax myrtle
        and giant blue

irises   Under the moon everything is new

Offshore   halos bead
        the bleary horizon

Even when the wind is hot

it's cool   the dollar weed and racachas
bind the levee   and the storm

passes
        like an archangel

Sandra Sarr

Siren

She was one of the best damn tassel dancers in New Orleans,

what some cat-called a sleazy heat-seeker, a holy hell-
raiser pacing the stage all glittery and shimmying, a regular

hard-core harlot, so says her ne'er-do-well daddy,

the back-door cash-taker.

Now, she chases flames, not to stoke, but to extinguish,
a truck, not tassels, the tool of her trade.
No one can drive like her, red blaze of speed, light flash,
and siren wail. She owns the driver's seat, watches both ways,

horn blaring and warning *Get out of my way!*

Town men, they're still chasing her fire truck.
Some nights, in silence, she hears one man's old code-knock

on her door. He meets her in dreams. Those nights
she awakens with a trace of a smile and lights a Lucky Strike.

Mona Lisa Saloy

Lincoln Beach

My sister took us little ones to
Lincoln Beach, the Negro beach on
Lake Ponchartrain, site of 3000 mini-me kids laughing.
Every city had one then, us
Catching the Galvez, then the Franklin Ave bus, next the
Little Woods bus, connecting us to
Haynes Blvd at Lincoln Beach. Seemed
Like we went to another Parish!
No car
Daddy said busses work fine, and
Walking is good for the soul, and
He didn't want the debt or become chauffer; he'd
Rather have family over on Sundays for
Backyard get-togethers
Cracking oyster shells for
Po-boys on French bread from Dixiana bakery or
Boiling crawfish till ruby red and cayenne pepper hot, like the
Sun beaming blindly in summers
On the way to and home from Lincoln Beach
We sang Smokey Robinson or Back Water Blues. We slept
We kissed the bus windows
Ducked white-folks stares
Squeezed into seats in the
Back during jim crow. We
Packed lunches, a few *plarines*,
Creole home-made candies for treats. We
Walked my first sand on the man-made beach
Swam in the BIG pool, me, no bigger than the kitchen table
Jack-knifed off of the high dive! Then, we
Fell asleep like bricks once home

Lincoln Beach. Our Beach, now
Decayed and deserted like old jim crow laws, but
Standing barely, crippled since closed, then we
Took our cash to Ponchartrain Beach, the
White beach park, also gone, now a
Technology center just off the university, the
Black side of the Lake road still not as polished as the
Other side near the Marina lined with yachts
Wouldn't notice if it weren't so. Now, some of our youth
Kill each other wholesale for sport, some fake fantasy or
Dead Rapper's dream of guns and glory, and they
Take no peace in bus rides, only lust for
What they don't own, want, have only a hand out, "gimme . . . .
God help us, and may peace pour plenty

Ed Ruzicka

It Is Raining Again

For Lucy Blu

The soft rain, the bare ticks from clouds
too heavy to contain themselves anymore.
Sometimes in New Orleans it is hard to tell
the difference between a cry of joy, a cleansing cry
and someone who just came here to give up
as they gasp out grief in an alleyway or in a bar.
Laughter is close behind the pain here. Or ahead of it.

Anyway, rain is ticking onto statues of generals,
statues of musicians, onto pigeons whose orange
claws brighten. Silver chains of rain slink
into the sewer or pool in low spots on asphalt.
Trickles dive off rooftops down long links
of copper gutters, spill onto the sidewalk

as lovers pass. Rain sidles down
where the many-colored pigeons
bathe in a shimmer of puddle.
As pairs head back to hotel rooms
of urgency and joy, an older couple
sits under an awning. Their love
exactly as it is here, intact
while they sip, pass a warm cup slowly,
back and forth, hand often touching hand.

Pomegranate Poem #1

In the wanton spirit of wanting to spit
in the face of Asian detachment,
at a garden party ten years back,
an obscenely see-&-be-seen kind of scene
at some reverse-snob's shotgun shack,
I bit into that pomegranate,
feeling it my duty to embrace original sin, that it's the poet's
proper place to throw himself, at every opportunity,
under the wheels of the juggernaut.
Therefore—to adopt yet another metaphor—I got
& remain from-asshole-to-appetite reamed
upon a spit of (yup) pomegranate wood
to such an extreme that I cannot pick up a pen to tackle
a poetic theme without hearing the crone's cackle
& groan at my audacity, & similarly, in my erotic dreams,
someone or something always intervenes
to thwart consummation
so that I've come at last to say, with, it's
my hope, a modicum of the hard-fought
grace of a Chief Joseph or Roberto Duran, *No mas*,
striving thereby to redeem anathema
& placate the wrath of Our Lady of the Pomegranates.

Caroline Rowe

1. The Fool

Oh fuck a job and money.
My skeleton sings in the fire.
No pot to boil coffee
for this new lover in
but he makes even thirst
sweet as the ribbon
strangling my hair
like the tramp's bindle,
tangled shut
and mostly empty
for the journey—
my God, we're off...

No more dope.
I'm gonna be straight now
like I've been threatening.
Against the old stove,
my hips are nothing,
a fractured vault,
murmuring of womanhood,
the brittle bone hood
of a shell.

But everything gets to be well again.
This dawn intends
as usual, to be new.
Its celestial cipher
spins in my eyes.
I bob like a balloon.
Gravity unties
its strings.

No fitted sheet.
The bed's bower is barren.
No lamp to see me
undress in the dark.
No fifty cents for bus fare.
I'm fine on foot.
The agreeable femur
flesh thaws
in the white hound's jaws
that pull me back from the edge
of love's cliff
like a frenzy of angels.

No food.
No education.
I can't retain a damn thing
but abide
the orders of all suffering—
love, little wickedness,
live with your evil luck.
and fuck it, let me be
a dumb and gentle
self-immolation to joy.
I'm not ashamed of anything
since I've died.
Faith is stupid
but it's all
I got by my side.
If Christ wasn't
a fool,
he'd have never been crucified.

Denise Rogers

A Loss (a poem in the voice of my mother)

in memory of Edward Recar

There was a time,
before I lost my French,

I knew enough
to sing with tunes
my grandpa crooned.

I remember being four
and spoiled with many sweets.

He toted me
upon his back
around the gallery.

***

We'd end up in the kitchen
at the corner pantry shelves

where I would root around
to my small heart's content.

I liked the pictures of the kids
on cookie tins and apple cans.

He said one day I'd have my own;
I'd frown and shake my head

as he would laugh
and then we two
would put them back again.

***

One year I got the influenza bad.
He wrapped me up
and drove us
down the lanes.

My mom had lost
three boys before,
Roy and Floyd
and David,
None of whom I ever knew.

***

It seems all wrong
he has no stone,

nor iron cross
to mark the place he lies.

My daddy paced it off
for me, when I was fifteen,
from an old dogwood tree,

but now that tree is gone,
and all I know is
he's in Richwoods' churchyard there.

He died in summer.
I do remember that.

***

My uncles made the coffin
they put him in. They did their best.
Poor folks laid them out at home
still in those days.

I wasn't scared,
until I understood
and watched
my mother covering
our few mirrors one by one.

She said we don't want
his soul caught here at home,
do we?

    ***

When she found me
on a chair,
pulling all the pillowcases off,
she spanked me hard
and sent me out
into the yard.

I sat out on the gallery
and cried and cried all day,
knowing he never would have minded
if I'd wanted him to stay.

Matt Robinson

Disappeared

I remember postmarks on envelopes
and payphones on street corners,
I recall the sound of typewriters in offices
and polite elevator operators
in very old buildings

I remember cigarette smoke on airplanes
and cigarette smoke in restaurants
and the words "smoking or non-smoking"
posed an indifferent question,
not a verdict on sin and redemption

Once upon a time I sent my packages
and mailed my letters
from a grand Post Office
with carved mahogany paneling
and walls of numbered personal boxes
gleaming and heavy with permanence;

polished brass railings and doorknobs,
high ceilings and thick glass
casting sunlit sepia shafts
upon the marble floor below
even the air felt significant
like a courthouse, like a church;
a sacred way-station
for Grand Concepts
and Important Deals,
for Love Letters
and Past-Due Notices

but last week in an embarrassed building
of parking lot and concrete
with bullet-proof windows and nickel-plated latches
I purchased stamps
from a cubicle of institutional cloth
and plastic veneer
without so much as a splinter of wood in sight,
drab metal cold and grey
absorbing pallid fluorescence
from the overhead lights

but the people behind the counter
were professional and patient,
imperfect yet attentive
much like they used to be,
they told me to have a nice day as I left
and I think that they meant it
and it is good
that some things
have not disappeared

Brad Richard

The Rain

—for Tim

I need you to remember the rain—
        lie down with me, love, and remember
                all the rain we know, while we know;

how it talked to itself through afternoons
        like a boy with his imaginary playmate,
                rain lost to itself in its coming, as we listened;

how its burst down morning lawns
        ended bright-beaded on castor-bean leaves
                and in your hair when you came in with the dog;

how the hurricane pelted through the porch screen,
        as we sat naked there in the after-dark, heat
                heavy with wet, our slick skin one with night;

how sudden a fall—imagine you and me
        loosened from the sky, oblate,
                pancake-shaped, small wobbling

spheres cast down and finding
        in falling one another, falling in air
                as in one another, how, one body

spirited homeward, heavier
        in falling further, we're swallowed
                in earth's mouths.

Beverly Rainbolt

August 15, 2014

a month. it's been a month.

two months, a week, and a day ago the mri showed your brain still
free of lesions as it had been since march when they cut the grape-sized one out.

two months and a week ago you posted a photo
you and the boys at the pool; you were radiant,
the three of you smiling in the sun
you joked that you made a lousy marco polo "it."

two months and two days ago you enjoyed an end-of-school pool
party with friends and kids and lover—a summer of camps and vacations
planned out (as you would do).

two months and a day ago you went to your sister's birthday party.
your head hurt. i walked you home. slowly. you were still
getting your walking legs back i sat with you
in the dark a while, your eyes closed, you didn't feel
like talking.   *my body is tired*   you said.

two months and two days ago you started the new drug
that was supposed to save you   we had hope again.
eleven days later   a freight train of lesions
was roaring through your brain.
eleven days.

one month. it's been a month
since i left the hospice to take a shower
and you took your last breath

the next day was your birthday and
we were left to walk this landscape without you.

marking time becomes our ritual
  missing you   our mantra

Sarah A. Rae

My Mother, My Name

I have a laptop. In my laptop I write my poems.

I have a Toyota. In my Toyota I play CDs and sing and eat and drink coffee and drive.

I have postcards. Che Guevara smiles and smokes cigars and looks tragic and intense in the postcards.

I have my mother's ring. In my mother's ring the colors look like skies.

I have my grandmother's gold watch. The watch works erratically and the band is not original.

I have my worries. In my worries my mother dies and she does not know my name.

I have my pictures of boats at Puerto Angel. I took them myself.

I have my retro skirt. Orange and yellow and salmon and olive green and periwinkle blue collide in my retro skirt.

I have my flowered red rug from Morocco. My boyfriend said to use one of the sides

during the summer and one of the sides during the winter.

I have my mother. I have my name.

Jimmy's Shoes

He sits cross-legged, his blond hair a Rastafarian cascade,
His frail body half-disappearing in the fading light.
He looks worn out, beat down,
As torn apart by life as his jeans are by age.
It's the kind of thing you notice in a small crowd.
But when Jimmy begins to speak,
Cooing his tale in a voice as languid as a summer's eve,
A melody of words as sweet as wind in the reeds,
It's the kind of thing you forget.
You sit back, close your eyes and go where Jimmy takes you.
The tale ends when the hot ashes singe his fingertips.
The dry silence startles you and you look around,
Realize Jimmy and you are still here in this space.
The worn fabric of his jeans grabs your eyes
And you follow the trail of thread
To a pair of tennis shoes so old parts have fallen away.
There it is. There it is! The life, the truth of his tales.
There, in Jimmy's shoes.

Jonathan Penton

Heroic Man

Gaston Lachaise
British, born in France, 1882-1935
Bronze, edition 1/6
Gift of Syndey and Walda Besthoff, 2000.209
Installation funded in memory of Mrs. Richard W. Freeman

My skull is very small.
Everyone notices.
People describe me as having a wisdom of the body.
In some mouths, that means I'm beautiful.
In all mouths, that means I'm a fool.

Now I am scarred.
Covering one arm
both shoulderblades
down one scapula.
Now the wisdom of my body is keloid.
My skull no longer houses the windows to my soul.

Self-Portrait as 70s Childhood

I was just a latchkey kid roaming the cul de sac,
King Tut always on my mind. At holiday parties
I ate fondue and pretended it was my hand
controlling the blob in lava lamps. It has not
been proven otherwise. For one conceived
in a waterbed between fights, what can life be
but a conversation pit with a disco ball sun,
or a wood-paneled den with a wet bar
from which I steal sips of all liquors equally?
My favorite car is a van with a bed inside of it.
The floor is quicksand and macrame beards the walls.
Buddha candles light the way. My favorite
books are pocket-sized, from the checkout line.
Horoscopes and diets are all I know.

Lisa Pasold

Buttermilk Drop

for Ariel Gordon

by ladyparts you mean not the cunt but the great inner clockworkings of mystery and science—though I do love the word cunt—the come-hither hard swoop feel of it on the tongue and its place/absence in language—when what we mean—cunt—is admittedly wide-ranging

it's the word I didn't use on the phone long-distance twenty years ago—back when we still used landlines remember that was a thing—when I'd been pap'd without any sense of celebrity—then flew out to work—so I was in France when the results came in—I clutched that clunky beige receiver—speaking to the doctor's secretary through trans-Atlantic static—earnest in my panic I said *But am I gonna die?*

even now I am indeed amazed she didn't reply *Yeah, baby, you gonna die, sit down already*—but instead she lied—maybe because her momma told her sometimes you gotta do like a magician with those rabbits—that day she said *No, you not gonna die*

so now I can reassure you—so many years and two surgeries later—while eating a particularly delicious Buttermilk Drop - which is somewhat like a donut hole but with icing—isn't everything quasi-miraculous so far as it goes—that doctor's secretary was right—the ladyparts haven't killed me—though I understand what she meant back then was yet—what she was saying silently—was *Not yet, love, not yet.*

Andrea Panzeca

Twins

Weird how Connie Martin and Dad are both Pisces and twins.

Dad used to dream of Connie opening a tamale stand called Connie's Tamales.

My sister and I made up a song: *Connie's tamales, Connie's tamales.*

Tamales is close to *two males*, which if twins could be fraternal or identical.

Once I listened to *Louisiana Eats!* and Poppy Tooker interviewed a man whose grandmother made tamales at my grandfather's Bourbon street night-club.

La Lune, per the WPA, was "one of the more popular spots of the French Quarter" whose Mexican food was "excellent and reasonably priced."

My grandfather was friends with Enrique Alferez, Mexican artist and part of the WPA, who made reliefs of a moon for La Lune and Adam and Eve

for my grandparents' house, in New Orleans East, for their bar wall, in front of which, in a photograph, stood my dad and his twin Wilma.

Melinda Palacio

Letter to Time

I may be the last to linger,
but life's a ride worth living.
Thought I'd change the world,
but the world changed me.

Stale bread and a white flag, offerings.
Dear Time, pull back the dusty curtain.
No spell to quell this pain.
Do you see me?

I no longer play with toys.
The face that stares back at me is not my own,
but my mother's, my grandmother's.
Your lover Mictlan wins again. Always.

I may never understand your greed or
the thin place you've hidden away my youth,
how you kept the best years for yourself,
left me for lonely, almost dead.

Anthony Oscar

Family Violence

all-binding & eventually
the constriction of confusing embraces,
chasing the tides of love
chafing grips—do you know what an Indian burn is?
an Indian summer or an Indian gift

suddenly seeing codes in all sorts of communication
like a simple rule of thumb
& realizing a dog can be trained to do anything at all
when treated with scraps of meat

I've always been the wrong kind of mirror—
the one you want to break,
cursing their karmic protection
fearing powers beyond & through them
within every universal connection

& me? alone in my room trying
to point towards the vague sources
of torn or sliced ligaments
needing to be reattached,
but worried to go under for surgery
when doctors molest
unconscious patients without question

what hope does one have to walk again?
it's not always so serious, so heavy,
but when it is
                    o   o   o   p   h   h hh...
it gets hard to get up
& more start piling

Biljana D. Obradović

Catullus' Sparrows

a sestina for John

I heard the lemon merchant singing the song
"O Sole Mio," surrounded by tiny sparrows
looking for morsels of food beside lake
Garda on Sirmione, while I drank Bordolino wine
at the Piccolo Castello restaurant, ate a salad with olives,
with my grilled branzino, near the castle, after I swam

in Borgia Hotel's pool in my new pink swim-
suit I had bought at one of the stores where a song,
in Italian, came out of a radio next to the long, thin olive
dish plate I nearly bought if it weren't for the sparrow
which Petar, my son, saw, so that I ran out without the Bordolino wine
I had also meant to buy to drink before dinner by the lake.

Instead we went for a walk away from the lake
as the day was gorgeous. Later we wanted to swim
in the pool. There was a couple there drinking wine
(I don't know if it was Bordolino), listening to songs
in their ears, so as not to disturb the sparrows
following Petar's every move, standing on an olive

branch, while the swans could be seen beyond the olive
tree, swimming alone or in pairs on the lake.
Lizardo (how we named the lizard), climbed the rocks near the sparrows.
I watched him closely, making sure he was not near to where I swam,
but he was so small. He should be afraid of me, or the loud songs
coming out of a passing car below us, near the wine

store, where they also sell Grappa in shiny bottles unlike the wines.
Also made of local grapes, this strong pomace brandy, can go well with bread

    dipped in olive

oil, dipped, as an appetizer, or usually as a digestive after dinner, with music, a song,
after an espresso, perhaps in that restaurant with blue glasses right beside the lake.
There one evening a macho guy came with his fancy boat. Unable to swim
in this water, he parked, then brought his two ladies like a sparrow

perching himself in front of a crowd of other fancily dressed sparrows.
He sat down, ordered what must have been the best local wine,
then lit a cigarette, while the babes showed off swim-
suit like tops, with large, black necklaces, dressed all in olive
colored silk, glad they did not fall into the lake
getting out of the boat in high stilettos, as the band played their song,

the song of the privileged local sparrows who live near the lake
in the Grotte di Catullo, singing, like the poets, to the wine,
to the olive trees, as connoisseurs, before taking a swim.

Austin Nieli

Tantric Weather

We believe there is some mysterious power to the rain
and that we are absolved by it
that as we thought the day before
means nothing any longer
so long as it has washed away our wrongs
and by the morning dried and fed the universe well
We would like to think the tour guides
make less money for telling the truth
about New Orleans looking the most beautiful
when it is raining simply because the truth hurts
rather than the real truth,
that they make less money
when they believe the stories they tell.
Even to believe this isn't true means believing
that New Orleans is more beautiful when it is raining,
but the real truth is that, if you look closely enough,
if you were really there the night
the tugboat crashed into the Riverwalk
with hundreds of terrified tourists running for their lives
and it so happened to be raining,
you wouldn't stop to question any of this
and the tour guides wouldn't have the guts to say so.

Kay Murphy

Nude

Sitting in the vintage burgundy chair,
cat in arm, she wants to turn the pages with her tongue,
slide it over the lavender on the throat of Madame Bovary,

kiss the musk on the lips of Fra Grubach,
suck Bishop's thumb after throwing back the fish .
The long fur of the cat makes her nipples hard.

But when meditating, cat in lap, she can only be
the nothing that she isn't. The desire that isn't.
Rising, what she knows stays on the bean-filled cushion.

Sometimes the blinds are closed, sometimes not.
The young man next door stands under the carport,
leans on his pickup, smokes. The truck doesn't run.

She imagines he sees her, not on the cushion, not
in the chair, not with a cat but with her breasts
bare, letting him think he is the reason.

Geoff Munsterman

Good Looking Out

A genius can love you to ruin if he
hates himself enough, but don't let the episodic
madness of manics fool you: some fingers unlock
with gobs of paste the revelation of night's anatomy.
Some ears, through the overwhelming gloomth of
language droning—an endless alerting press
to our strike team's effectiveness & ads
praising foot fungi dying, both set to hits
from someone's youth—compose from a gospel
of sighing mouths already a century old
patches in the busted hulls of frayed ventricles.
When his country's army saw in his brother
& him a pair of promising snipers, he told them
Drop dead. Told me that someone selling you
your soul's death has breath stinking of petroleum.
Gods walking around thinking they were people
insulted him—deities twisted into pirates,
pack mules, pincushions. *You're not a boy*,
he hummed one floral morning, *you're a whale*.
I thought it was a fat joke. Still I struggle trusting
offering my reflection—to muse makes your brilliance
a weed casting shadows in someone else's valley.

Footnote found in biographies of the 20th century's
strangest & therefore most desirable muse, he
made tea for me the way she used to make for him
& into early morning hours chirped grinningly
about nights he offered his mouth as tribute
to her ancient nipple. Hours I watched awed

at him breaking his broken to almost powder
& with tears & spit mixing the broken into gobs
he'd patina with the oxidized residue of a bloody
thumb. Fucking his way through every stern-eyed
sculptor & full-hipped songstress this city
sirened to his studio, his attempts at playing
Velvet to their Nico meant he always only played
himself. For the months I chauffeured him
around New Orleans, learned his coffee,
transcribed mournful & important gibberish
from notebooks, napkins, scraps of magazines
in exchange for a patch of crammed studio
in Schneider from which my sweeping yielded
paint-marred floor where no nightmares gnawed.

Twice he took me to the river hoping I could learn
to breathe. When my mother took us for sandwiches,
his flat-falling charm made her worry for him until
the day he died & each time in the year since
when she forgets he died, her right eye wells
up thinking of his jaw just like her older brother
Danny who torched any years he could at Fat City
coke parties & grueling offshore gigs held until
a piss test ran him off & metastasis whittled him
to bone. Somewhere between
                              dying artists & dying
carpenters, I traded crying at grief or yawning
at exhaustion for sighs, silence, running from
the places that reveal themselves as no home:
                              wherever I am,
                    I never adhere.
Though I would never catch his genius or exhume
from within myself a tongue skilled at humanity,
I wrote something that made Herbert Kearney cry.

I am a whale who knows fire is a bellyacher.
It destroys with the merciless emptiness of a banker,
conquering army as bored by screams as they
are confused by weeping. My mother's tears

45

are saltwater. When Herbie cried his tears were
Sanskrit ballads wasted on whaleboys, weird
women, pincushion punks, & to the pirates
moored at the Julia Street wharves he was
a waste of talent too beastie too bawdy too
incongruent for commercial cashing-in-on.

No living person speaks his broken-hearted.

Benjamin Morris

Lies We Tell Tourists

That there is an alley
off Beggar's End where
the wind never blows,

that wisteria here never
blooms on a Tuesday.
We haven't seen a bird

in years, not since
the street war of the 80's,
when they sided with the mice

and the cats ran them all
out of town. That glass
does not shatter, it melts,

that our central library
holds millions of books,
most of them not yet written.

Our river was never a plague pit,
our dump never a parkland—
that our beautiful, beautiful city,

where the *trompe l'œil* oils the mind
sits just inside of fact, but falls
just outside of the eclipse.

Gail Morgan

My Mother's Mind

(The Physics of Light)

light is both a particle...

when my mother's mind was young
it was filled with the noise
of an abacus   sorting
and counting   empty
or full   yours
or mine
she was once a dancer
telling stories
of what she gave up
to marry
yet when my father
gazed at her
tasted her
with his eyes
I could hear the faintest
click of beads
as her body unspooled like
a ribbon
towards him

I made myself small
to watch as she sat
at her vanity   carefully penciling
her brows   powdering
her face   etching
her lips with a glistening tube
of Helena Rubenstein Apple Red
until they were plump and full

and perfect
then stood next to her
at the mirror   asking
if she thought my lips were pretty
but meaning what is it like
to be a woman
will anyone love me
will anyone want me
she said no
your lips are thin
I think they are much too thin

...and a wave

when my mother's mind was old
it no longer
sat in a straight-backed chair
but floated above her   listing
sideways
my father murmured
it's getting much harder to control her
she doesn't do
what I tell her do
she can't think of the words
she wants to say
she doesn't always
know who I am

we sit together she and I
I lift my camera and ask
if she remembers dancing
to the music
my father says
she doesn't really care for music
but my mother waves her hands through the air
like a bird
like a feather
like early June
don't take pictures of my hands she whispers
they are old and ugly

I say no
your hands are beautiful
I think they are very beautiful
she stares at me long enough
that I can hear the sound of her mind weeping
how sweet   she says
how very sweet you are

Marian D Moore

Found On The Street

A bullet
two inches long
brass,
scarred,
resting in the
crevices of this
summer sidewalk.
This one, at least,
broke no mother's
back;
no father's
sanity;
its absent
brothers
not there
to speak for themselves.

Z. W. Mohr

The Bone Fire

From the old words
For what we often do
To ward away the dark;
Throw those old bones
Into the fire,
Make a bone fire
To ward away the shadows
Of old loves,
And passion's demons.
Let them burn into the darkness
Until we're warmed by them,
And the future grows brighter.
Build that bone fire,
Never keep the skeletons of loss around
To taint new love's hallowed ground.
Put them in the fire, love,
And let them burn
Until your heart is free.
The bones of their fingers,
That once wrapped around yours.
The bones of their shoulders
You used to brush your lips across.
The bones of their legs,
That wrapped around you.
The jaw bone that used to kiss you
Sweetly in the morning light.
The bones of their arms,
That used to hold you tight.
The bones of their hips,

That used to hold you in their sway.
The bones of their ribs,
That used to writhe beneath your embrace.
Those bones that haunt our hearts.
The bones that keep us from connecting
To another's bones.
Take those bones and burn them.
Throw them in the bone fire.
Build a blaze,
And kiss the one's you love by the fire.
Let those bones just burn away.

Monica Carol Miller

Ornithology

I found myself watching wrens in my patio garden,
Hopping between the pots, dianthus to zinnia.
I hung a bird feeder next to the baskets of petunias,
Fully embracing the middle aged hobby as my gray grew.
First the cardinals came. They mate for life:
An auspicious sign, a friend assured.
Then bickering finches, whose flying is
More a controlled fall from the balustrade.
I woke to a patchwork towhee banging at the window,
A morning Cathy loudly seeking Heathcliff.
My favorites, the Carolina warblers
Leap to the highest railing to sing on the windiest days,
Their eye makeup less like my mountain cousins than Divine.

Rainwater

Is it raining? Mother asks, the fresh
desert air cooling the room at dusk.
Raindrops tap tap the windowpane.
From her bed, she calls for a moist cloth
to cool her forehead. *Go outside,*
she whispers, *put some rainwater*
on it, she says, because her head aches
and her heart is so tired. I step into
the storm, then bring her a rainwater-cool
cloth, to drape over her brow.

That night, I dream she is part of
a special project where she leaps
into the roiling ocean and a golden
retriever rescue dog swims to her,
tows her to shore. She is proud
of herself and I am proud of her.

Someday, my mother will become rain
water, to evaporate and rain down,
evaporate and fall over New Mexico mesas.

I awake, relieved by clear, lapis
skies and her solid figure awaiting
my damp kiss.

Mike Marina

The Drop

It's never as dramatic
As some make it out to be
It starts with something innocuous
A flipped circuit
    a confusion of floor commands
    A power surge
Imbalance of weight and torque
I never notice until everything
    stops

Except for that damned muzak
Plucking pianos spitting out
  Somber notes as
silence begins to mingle with stale air
and suffocates all open space
  I stop hearing sounds
    Everything replaced by muffled gurgles
Weightless, my feet feel heavier than ever before
My lungs expand, crushing my ribs
No longer sure if physics is working
Did I break the universe?
Or did I just break?

That piano keeps playing
  I sink inch by inch
Sweat cooling my back
  While carbon dioxide burns my lungs
How much air do I really need anyway?
  Who needs lungs anyway?

Why breathe?
Why bother?

The muzak incessantly drones on
    I hear "I love you" sung from the speakers
Hear it turn into static, simple noise
And those words used mean so much to me

My hungry tongue begins to swallow my words
My cries for help get locked in the crypt of my jaw
No syllables phoenix enough to save me
The floors creep by
Slowly
Grinding gears echo
The hollow groans escaping my throat
    I might not make it
Years slip by and I slip further down
How far will I drop?
My dead jaw murmurs dirges to my dying ears
The muzak keeps playing, playing, playing
Buffering me from the silence
Gripping my throat

My depression was like a broken elevator
    I couldn't leave
Nearly overwhelmed by the massive nothing
I was halfway in the basement before I crawled out
I have never looked at elevators the same way since

Monica Mankin

Where Rivers Begin

The sky mines its way in
through the rain, tiny rills

bore up from the earth
to meet at the surface.

"The mind is a river"
sister says, "Mine split

from an ax,"
but axes can't split rivers

and she will never say
what actually happened.

She spits her soupy chaw
over the guardrail

into the muddy brown waters
below, and I know

before the ax hit
she was not a river.

She was a girl dreaming
of a girl turned evergreen.

Her mind like that haven
of a tree but not weeping,

not yet seeking an escape
from a man's whetted blade.

Then one day she took scissors
to her neck, cut two shapes:

one a belligerent's raging song,
her current too strong for the swim;

the other she thinks no one sees,
pulling away until it swamps

among the cypress knees
steeping in the mud.

What cracks the voice
into trebled tones?

What divides the water?
That singular body

from which she was made,
salty and fresh, funneling

into and out of itself
into who she was before

and is after
here at the guardrail

holding on.

Monica Mahn

Saint/Street

Mercy is strained-estranged-arraigned in a never ending lemniscate. I woke up at 3AM to a cat licking my eyelid. I shivered but at least my eyes are free of flies and I think maybe even planks.

Next morning I pull in to the two floor parking garage- I park on the first and walk through the door on the back of the building. Elevator to fourth floor. Long carpeted hallway with windows that only look into waiting rooms, never escaping the building.

I open heavy glass door, talk to receptionist, get called into appointment. I tell the doctor about what happened to me. She tells me she's officially adding the letters St next to my name. I ask her what they mean. You've been through a lot, she says. I'm not sure whether it means I deserve sainthood for my persecution or just that I've been systematically crushed under the world's wheels for the sake of misplaced pragmatism alone.

Have you ever been to a place where it seems god did not finish creation? A mountain climbs towards the sky then suddenly drops off where he gets distracted. Rivers begin then are swallowed beneath the surface of the earth where he forgot to finish drawing a path for them.

Has it ever occurred to you that there might be people like that? Because sometimes I think I might be one of them.

Karen Maceira

Faith

I know my life is meant for something good.
Light lies upon the water where damselflies
hover and marsh roses bloom.

Father's father lays his hand, abiding shadow,
across my winsome heart, the grief a covenant
I can remand. My life is something good.

My brothers drown and sorrow creeps
from my mother's womb; my father, broken, weeps
while damselflies touch water and roses bloom.

The day you die with no goodbye
the surf gives up a moonflower's unlikely gaze.
I look into its steady eye: my life is something good.

For being's a song whose words I know,
whose music plays within the waves,
the soundless wing of damselfly and blooming rose.

A mariner now of memory, I search
for damselflies, marsh roses,
light upon the spirit, a soughing sea.
I know my life is meant for something good.

Martha McFerren

One Is One: 2020

1

I've been indoors so long
my skin has lost all color
though my hair remains
bright, unnatural red.
It's the Lady Lazarus look.

Is it permissible these days
to be so disgracefully white?
A dark sheik in shadows
singing beneath the window
in that 1920's romance.
Pale hands I loved
beside the Shalimar.
Am I glowing from within
like Cypriot alabaster?

2

No decent food is delivered
in our neighborhood, unless
you count bizarre combinations
from the vegan pizzeria.
My husband, who cooks daily,
longs for printed menus
and people who refill your glasses.

I thumb through Nordic cookbooks,
craving Danish open-faced sandwiches

like the ones I ate in Iceland.
Even if we escape this house,
Iceland will ignore us. We will not
be summoned again to smorgasbord.
No smoked herring for me.

3

I'm on-line buying clothes
for parties no one is giving,
clothes too young for my throat.
My closets are tins packed tight
with pastel sardines.

Free to roam, I'd still be odd
wearing these dressy florals
in a culture of denim and hoodies

I've bought too many books,
and written too much about
the stuff in books, yet not enough
to justify their purchase.
Crossing the floor, I dodge
stacks of volumes, all mewing,
Read me. Read me.

And why this sudden desire
to collect Limoges boxes?

4

I'm contacting everyone
in my battered address book,
anyone who isn't honestly dead.

Lost Friend: I'm stuck here
and was stuck long before
this virus crept into us.
Sickness? Depression?

Broken bones? All the above.
I'm sorry, I should have written,
even though pursued by crows.

Twenty years ago, I was
sick of hearing from you
and cringed when I saw your
trademark scarlet ink.
Now I miss your familiar bitchfest.
Phone me, I'll listen now.
I'll ask about your persistent children.
Damn you, tell me I'm loved.
Remind me I once lived.

Cameron Lovejoy

[untitled]

                    (I suck
          solemn lemons
when life gives them

              cruel ulcer in the cheek

bell curve of the tongue

                didn't always nobody
       talk existence   a singed design

                     on the ass

       the war is so raw in the news today
                          sewn

              my eyes shut

fart a raft cast away to edit tides

                   one virus
          interfuses with another   crisis after

christmas of course IPAs are racist look

at gasoline—

          then someone
              introduces some reductions: a cup

sugar cayenne an arctic
cube I am a cub

                        puckering in his high

chair—back then   when the deltas lasted)

Daniel W. K. Lee

Where the Sidewalk Ends

In New Orleans, beast and banquette yield
to the Southern live oaks' splayed hips.
The concrete, jumbled as though branches—
gloved with resurrection fern—had pried up
and tossed slabs aside like mahjong tiles.
I bet those trees howl to their roots
at the human animal and our resigned governments
("no point to new pavement"), telegraphing
their glee beneath South Carrollton Avenue,
swaying to fake a breeze, mocking our gullibility.
And what more than strange fruit persuaded them
long ago of our pitiful hubris, our banal arrogance?
Generations named for whatever comes after Z
will expire before the dendrochronologists,
marveling at a clean slice of trunk like a Christmas ham,
count its growth rings to determine age of death,
its widest zero, its number of fucks left.

Bill Lavender

from: *city of god**

museum of capital - for norman fischer

the city of god is a painting in the
museum of capital, which lines the walls of the capitol—
you can tell the difference because the o looks
like a dome, my 4th grade teacher told me, a few
years back, though the capital with an a attempts
to swallow the conceptual field by encircling
the building with its city meaning, as opposed
to its rural ($) meaning, where you might say
monsanto takes the place of town, having found
a way to charge interest on capital it never had, never
even had to borrow, seed money, so to speak,
growing from nothing to feed the world, somewhat
less bucolic than *agnus dei* days, at least
here, in america, and it wasn't that long
ago i was in the italian tyrol up the hill
from ezra pound's castle, we were taking
the funicular to the restaurant at the top
and just as we were pulling into the station saw
in the almost vertical pen beside us a little lamb
who looked up & baa'd as we passed and we said
how quaintly european without it occurring to our
quaint american consciousness till we got inside
and looked at the menu that she was it, reified, fet-
ishized object of market forces, listed at 'market price,'
fluctuations being too volatile, apparently, to allow
the number to be committed to print, a ghostly thing
like the ownership of the grain that fed her
and her mom, for ownership grows increasingly
abstract as the capitol dome gets more and more

often misspelled, and we paid for her abstractly, with a card,
never noting the actual price, just up the hill from where
the author of 'with usura' came to lay his head, still
hard in those days, on the cold castle stone, after
his daughter mary bailed him out of st. elizabeth's,
before the author of 'kaddish' made his pilgrimage
and the hard head softened, pulled down its vanity a
bit before sighing its last, now as certain as he had
been of his place among european capitols that it
had all been a botch, which of course it was...
and i keep looking for similar conversion in my current
fascist object of inquiry, ie augustine, who likewise
had a pretty line or two but was way more comfortable
spitting *simultas* than *caritas*, or indeed the current benito
wannabe getting botoxed in mar-a-lago, de facto capitol
of capitalism, lavish museum to its schmaltz, but see no
signs of conversion (unless in the language of capital we
mean by 'conversion' 'theft') in either, in which clever
referential fashion augustine proves himself correct
that the city of capital will always surround the capitol &
though the city of god may hang on its wall there will
be a price tag on it

city of god is a series of poems based on readings of the Augustini de civitate Dei,
The City of God by St. Augustine of Hippo, c. 420 AD, juxtaposed against current
events beginning Jan. 6, 2021.

Justin Lacour

Monday, 5:53 p.m.

This is a fairy tale where the
hero is more fascinated by
the witch, and so, the princess
sleeps and sleeps, the forest
of briars around her growing
thicker and thicker till the
original point of the story
is obscured, then forgotten.

I wish I could stay in this story,
but WWNO is playing Berg's
Violin Concerto,
transporting me back to
the summer I sat in the cafe,
each morning, pretending to read.

This was also the summer
every third song at the Pink
Pussycat Strip Club was either "Smooth"
or something off Rob Zombie's
solo album. The summer
strippers lap-danced
behind folding walls.
The summer an uncle
gave me a bobblehead
doll of Justice Scalia and told
me to stop being so sad.

Jonathan Kline

The Buddha of Bela Lugosi

When we were children
In the summer
in Petoskey
7 or 8 six-year-old boys
would run to the widowers for candy
We had a route
first to the m&m man on the corner
to stuff our pockets till he hollered
Pepcid gum from the mail man
and hard candy ribbons
from the veterans watching soaps
with tinfoil bows on the rabbit ears
but only Pauly and I would go to the big brown house
where the silent butler would answer the door
and let us in
The old man would give us each three spicy gumdrops
They were for adults
We could tell
grimacing at the cinnamon, clove, and sassafras
But we came everyday
to wait at the edge of the Persian carpet
 in that dark
carved-oak cave
for the birdcage elevator gate to open
And the gaunt tall man in his in his ash-gray suit
and cane
to say, "Hello boys, would you like a gumdrop?"
He kept them in his pocket
and placed them in our hands like sugared jewels

as the old man gazed at us
smiling in his frailty like the Buddha of Bela Lugosi
Pauly and I never said a word
We clutched our foul-tasting treasure
making our escape like thieves
never waiting for the butler

Dwain Kitchel

Smiles   (accepted by Orphic Lute)

Smiles are used for many tasks
to show, to kill, to soften
but i find the ones that please me most
are those that come most often

Jason Kerzinski

Blood Orange

I grow wildly
no longer thorned
concerned with commotions from above
the same old debate
is the world black and white or just shades of grey

I the roots of a blood orange tree
wait the arrival
a warbler singing a morning medley
a swarm of buck moths nipping at my leaves
a pair of hands caressing my skin

With life lines shaped like my intricate roots
hovering over my branches
caressing my ripe sunset colored skin
deciding if I'm ripe to pick

Julie Kane

Men Who Love Redheads

You can pick one out in a crowd
by the way he jerks his head
when an Irish setter passes,
drawn to that shade of red;
or the pickup line he utters
even to Raggedy Ann:
"If all your freckles merged,
do you know you'd have a tan?"

There are times you miss the clues
till you wake up after sex
to behold the nightstand photo
of his red-haired kids and ex;
then you know, for all of your charms,
he was only caught in the pull
of that least-known force of physics,
as a red flag draws a bull.

Some obsessives like girls plump
or missing a limb or two,
but the men hung up on redheads
are the men who prey on you.
Compared to men as a whole,
their numbers are very small,
yet without their kind in the world
you might never get laid at all.

Rodger Kamenetz

The Canceled Wedding

I wanted to write a song.
Underneath the song another song.
Underneath and so on. Song.

In the bottom box was a ring
To marry the whole world.
No — to betroth.

When I say *regret* I feel it in two bones.
One runs around my eye.
The other down my arm.

When I feel regret with two bones
It ends all wedding plans:
Weddings of blood and bone.

No one saw you as blood
In your white dress.
No one saw me as bone.

The tiniest diamond holds all praise.
It hides in the bottom box
where regret does its damage.

Sandra Johnson

Waiting

I'm waiting
        in my locked chest
        in my wound too tight clock
waiting for the tremor
for the throb
of the knob
        turned.
for the click back
of the no locks
on doors.

I'm prone on the block
waiting for the shot
from the barrel
waiting for the shock
to release me
to be made in water.
to ecstatic swim
as salmon
up
to sail
into the mouth
of the bear.

I'm daily fishing the paddle
from its lingerie nest
dropping my drawers
humming
waiting to be her task next

to be
the songbird shamed
to not
sing
in the talon.

Bolt upright
in night
I'm waiting on a cleaving.
for the cut that makes a rut
for his leaving.
forcing hands where I may
      If I make him now
      I won't wonder
      when he will.

Forgetting
always forgetting
to tell a stranger
"everything will be alright"
as our plane falls from the sky.
To remember that any moment
can be broken
by a sudden act of beauty.

Skye Jackson

i have only been back in new orleans for 2 weeks

when i learn about the 3 children
that fell into the river + drowned
trying to save each other

when they found the girl in Slaughter
rotting in 12 years of her own filth
under the watchful eyes of her parents

when 6 people were shot at a bar on magazine st.

when three children dragged a woman to death in mid-city
when the DA decided to try those three children as adults

when i sat in city park, having crawfish & strawberry mead
and my best friend asked me
why i took him back
but not if i was happy now

when i kept putting off quitting a job i hated

when he texted me from new york
saying he needed me
to come back

when the mayor sent out her condolences
when she did it again the next day
and the next

when i told my mama they needed

to put the parents of the rotting girl
under the jail

but they didn't even arrest them
until almost four months later

when one of the bodies of the drowned children
washed up on the mississippi river bank
when the three year old got shot on burgundy
when the mayor offered more thoughts
and prayers

when my best friend asked me over cocktails
at the hotel st. vincent:
skye why won't you just come home

and i ask myself
skye why don't you just come home

       i hear myself telling her:
       i never left

and now i don't know who to believe

Raymond "Moose" Jackson

miracles of st. roch

we went to st. roch's to read the bones
and ask questions that almanacs had no answers to
with the gates open
you could finally stand in the place of the dead
and appreciate the unsugared finery
of a barbaric centurion

an older, wiser altar boy
was given to us as a guide
his fingerprints worn smooth
by soft red bricks

not the usual sort of guide
pontificating facts and figures
pimping legends...
he just left us alone
        and caressed the stones

they say dead men tell no tales
but you know in new orleans that ain't true
all they do is chatter
sun up to sun down
and if anybody comes to sit a spell
they get an awful earful

and the only problem i have with the dead
is that they're a little obsessed with the past
(overhearing their talk of storms, i figured
they were ranting about katrina, but they

were still on about betsy)
and it is a very circuitous path
getting around to the subject of future

      but they do know
      reminds the altar boy
      in their scatterbrained way

they keep the prosthetics there as encouragement;
      your miracle is due

so if you go there
carry patience in your heart
remember that time is different
when you're stacked six generations deep

and pay regards to the gatekeeper
      you're sure to see him again one day

Arden Eli Hill

Star

I used to be the most lost boy on the island.
I used to be a mermaid in a pool sunk
deep in the jungle where sunlight
glinted off of a madman's hook
and the air was bright with
fairy dust falling
like pollen
on my chest
on the wolf teeth I wore with a leather strap
on my breasts not bound with seashells
on the kelp-streaked curve of my hips.

I used to climb
incredible heights of schefflera
and part strangler fig
to look at the world beyond
the blue-on-blue of sky and water.

I used to dive in clear lagoons,
swallow pearls for pleasure,
part my hair, and surface
to mock cannon fire and gold-lust.

Now, there is a deep amnesia
pressed against my temple
a migraine cocked and loaded
too much salt to breathe.

Carolyn Hembree

April 2020, New Orleans

> *That hem hath holpen whan that they were seke.*
> —"The General Prologue," *The Canterbury Tales*

Not big on pilgrimages, yet this fever drifts
from house to house. One leaky pirogue, adrift,
empty, listing to one side, on the bayou.
I look inside my neighbor's yellow house—joy
of a yellow house, shades up, rainbows chalked
on the walkway under a palm's moving shade,
palm where wild parrots roost. I play like
it's mine: my neighbor's breakfast nook, the playpen,
a last cold bite. A friend was topping off my glass
last night when a rolling violin solo, a show tune,
woke me. Here *prone* is transitive: to roll the sick
onto their stomachs so they breathe. Transitory strings
receded down the avenue. Above night transit,
lighter now, night birds sang—yes, we hear you again.
I sang along: *Maskmaker, maskmaker, make me . . .*
not a carnival mask on one you don't know you know
until they're in you: breathy sobriquet, dark alcove,
The Quarter. No, the other kind of mask so we breathe
for centuries, alone. Today I walk through another April
shower under April canopies where my thoughts
footnote old lines, *Whan that April . . .* Parish pilgrims
arrive on winds, on foot, by bike, by car, by bus,
by streetcar. Nowhere to be, no intercessor, I
join them. We roam the neutral ground, weeping,
scrolling news on screens that light our masks
so many magnolia petals, our hair the wind scrolls.

Ava Leavell Haymon

Replay Yesterday

was it the eyebrow pencil?   no
was it the azalea cuttings?   no
my owl nightlight?   no
rutabaga for dinner? too weird?
too much cream?   no
the wrong Allen wrench,
losing the bigger one?   no
oh, god, not the armadillo joke?!
no, don't be silly
the odometer, I'll bet?
no, stop guessing and think
Sara's measuring tape? that outfit?
her story of the camping trip?
you're not even close. Give up!
NO—not the chipped coffee cup, surely?
not recommending the article,
the one about Syria?   no
did I talk too much about geology?   for once, no
my school teacher grammar—how sometimes
that puts people off? not my smallish teeth?
tendency to interrupt? the way
I disagree with everything?

David Havird

Hurricane-Proof

That rasp—the ceiling fan?
Or rats? At night rats climb the palms,
the manager said. Don't sleep
with the doors to the balcony open. Besides,

sea wind's salt; everything metal
it rusts. She rapped the glass—
Paloma-proof! . . . The AC whooshes on.
In your mind's eye Paloma's heap,

twisted siding, splintered boards,
ragged sheetrock, glass-toothed muntins—fix
though you would that eye
on birds (blue sky, white loops of flight),

white baton tails
and narrow blades of black-tipped wings
and orange beaks (strain though you do
to train your ear on their reedy chirps),

beside the limestone bluff whose seams
they jet into and nest within—
that season's rental
bulldozed off, the concrete slab

scraped clean . . . Or hold in view
(the AC cycling off, that rasp!),
the morning's yellow-crowned night heron
toeing on yellow marsh-reed legs

the lip of the pool and piercingly
eying—there, it stabs, beaks up,
with that black beak which spears
the crabs that cloister themselves

in a salvage of shells
from the locals' harvest of sea snails,
a gurgling throatful of water—
red hermits amassing at sundown

under the fronds where you, the two of you . . .
It was as though the sunset,
while it impassioned you and this other
snoring beside you, whose sleep is

hurricane-proof,
hemorrhaged claws, a tide
that armored itself in spiral shells
for its incursion inland.

Ashley Mace Havird

Gone to Wild

Not like young folk—manic kids or feverish teenagers—
but old women, those I knew back when I wasn't one.
Great-Aunt Millie, "the pretty sister," my grandmother sniffed.
Sly-eyed, secrets pushing to sprout from her tight-lipped smile,
her cheek to my kiss a pollen-dusted rose.
Or my best friend's thin too-friendly Aunt Irene,
teeth stained red (her lipstick wandered),
whose fingertips, new-growth tendrils of jasmine,
grazed our arms if we got too close.

Or the ones whose names I've long forgotten—
cousins twice, thrice, who knows how many times removed—
who never missed reunions at Antioch Baptist Church.
Dressed to the nines in sky blue, peach, mint green, lilac,
hair spun and sprayed into fine and fluffy clouds,
they won all the door prizes: Oldest Descendant,
Traveled Farthest, Perfect Attendance.
Chatting among themselves, notes rising, falling,
depending on whether or not they wanted you to hear.
Tearing up generously, equally, at drooling babies
and toppled headstones in the gone-to-wild graveyard.

I picture them rooted, both garden and gardeners,
pruning, feeding, clawing up weeds in a fury.
Their perfume reeled me in.
Arms strong from the hoe—how else to explain such force?—
squeezed me to stalk-stiff corset or peony-cushioned bosom.
They weren't about to let go.

Nancy C. Harris

Dutch Boy's Finger

> *"Over again I feel thy finger and find thee"*
> —Gerard Manley Hopkins

I inhabit a pink shotgun
on a bend of the mississippi's mouth.
it engulfs me like an amoeba or jonah's whale,
intestinal home

whose windows blink in rhythms of prisms
& colored bottles: hamlin's wizard oil,
brown ginger tonic, blue bromo-seltzer,
hood's sarsaparilla—cure any ailment
of body or spirit:
rubber & jade & pencil plants, peacock feathers
snake images, stashes of unused poems, mardi gras beads—
aggregations of my objective life.

my sun registers in the earth
container of things
while air ascends & pulls
me apart stretching
endlessly my rubber ego
& only a fingertip keeps its midpoint
from giving out.

the weight of these things presses me down
like ocean waves' impersonal tonnage
& trying to breathe is as impossible
as getting out of bed, as Diane Wakoski said
'I want to go to sleep and never wake up'—
but dreams are just as troublesome & more real.

an ex-lover's ghost glimmers against these walls
as shadows cast from the blue blue scented genie lamp
& up on the levee dutch boy
plugs the hole w/ his finger—
divine finger owning a saint's patience
a buddha's third eye.

the philosopher's stone must be this finger
if he takes it out
the world will turn insideout, expelling
& shriveling like a balloon or a stomach.

being outside is unbearable.
on the streetcar
a man in a gray flannel suit touches
my blue-jeaned knee.
the mailman returns me to the book of the month club
& a file of cockroaches follows me to the river
unfooled by my piping, flawlessly alive.

dutch boy, just keep your finger in
this pied world
or the molecules will all fly off like blackbirds
unlimiting things
unfitting kings.

dutch boy, when you touch me
are you holding me back
or letting me out?

dutch boy, you could scour my doorstep
w/ your trigger finger.

Kelly Harris-DeBerry

For the Women Who Save Me

and pull me up for air,
covering me in blankets of honey

setting my table with a vase of mirth
bringing fruit baskets and soup

to the lips of my children.
They come through doors

made from long-ago intuition,
daughtering me like their own.

The women come knowing
the scent of hard times

grating worry into bowls
shaping meals by hand.

The women come ready,
washing loads of my business

folding me back into place.
These women, stiff lovers

demand my sorrows
on polished silver.

They come, disciples
of their mothers

grandmothers
field workers,

shucking tears
like corn.

Pressing my hard head
into pearl.

The women come,
in the rain, after work,

in the midnight,
to rock my regret to sleep.

They come, fussing,
and broken, washing

my face with compassion,
patching my heartbreak

with laughter.
Guarding my name

with candlelight.
They come saged,

conjuring ancestors
with Yoruba songs

and oiled blessings.
The women come

in dreams and flesh
as pregnant armies

with grenades of love
and sharp warm eyes

filled with visions
of daughters saving themselves.

George Guida

It's Just Like in the Old Days

when we had less scenery
and thought nothing of it.
Nothing about dew on blossoms.
We had fewer hours in the day.
Mornings went by
before the sun thought to reach us,

when we lived without floorboards.
Everything was light as air.
The air smelled of gardenias.
We didn't know where they were
growing and didn't care. After that
all we smelled was roses. But now
we're starting to smell gardenias again.

It's just like in the old days,
except petals fall from the sky.
One day is a fragrant shower,
another an aromatic storm.
The walk is blanketed with dying beauty.
Years back we would have swept it clean.
Now work like that is for the wind.

Anya Groner

Opinion Page

Poetry isn't dead. It just needs a haircut
and to close its mouth when it smiles

so we don't see its teeth. There're too many
feelings. Cut out the feelings. Ditto,

the facts. What poetry wants is a week
at the beach, a good tan, shrimp scampi,

and cocktails that glow UFO-green.
From the lawn chair, it'll see the horizon

is flat and the ocean is empty. Below
this surface is simply more surface,

which is why there's no need to splash.
What I hate most are insights. Yellowed

and wolfish, they remind me of riddles
I once read to my sweetheart. We shared

a beer float and studied the clues:
whiskey, a rope, fine china, and rings.

Later we wept and returned, unenlightened,
to a home we adored, pancakes and coffee,

headaches and naps. We had jobs and a bed,
joint checking and pills. Our love was a sentence,

two fools and a dog, some verbs and a mood,
and we like it, un-poetic, diagram-able, routine.

John Gery

In Clear Disarray

Count me out. The nation speaks
    in tongues the president does not
begin to understand.
Nor do I. My funny bone creaks,
    throat sore from the polyglot –
and payouts have stained my hand

green. Reading puts me to sleep,
    lulled by reassurances
I'll die before the entire
dream collapses in a heap
    of glass and telephone wire.
For others, the best chance is

not to seize the day, nor es-
    cape, nor even commit
suicide (as for Plath, Rimbaud,
and Socrates) but, *noblesse*
    oblige, retreat to one side
until the air clears, with no

ambition, until, like those
    extraordinary voices
I'm listening to right now
proliferating like trees,
    they rearrange all our choices
deciduously, somehow.

Elizabeth Garcia

Unplanned Certainties

Another random Monday night
this moment
an oakwood bar
with a 22-lifetimes-old man at the end
holding port-red blood-wine bottle & asking-
"How many full moons happen in one year?"
& if you know the answer
the one that allows life on Decatur St to
roll gently into dawns of twilight
he shares a glass or two with you & your
tired weak soul knowing all too well that
life for you will not gently roll & that life is
longer harder than you've thought it to be.
Then, in uncertainty of all time, a cooler,
sweeter moment blows in off the River
across slated rooftops, holding, pushing, pressing down
New Orleans Soulghosts long-since-gone
& passed through bloodied bone life strainers made
of stolen burnished steel—
& how many full moons happen in one year
to make your tired soul sing or cry regret & fear
of not living your life to perception that is your own
or of what others see you to be—
& at that point in the randomness of Monday night you meet up with
the Englishman Musician whose Surgeons have given him
5 years then 2 years after spleen & kidney have been removed
& who takes his clothes off looks in a mirror & closes his eyes
at reflection of Life in Death & Death in Life
& how many full moons happen in one year to make his soul

sing or cry with what is left, what is left, when Jesus Christ
is not the man at the end of that long oakwood random night bar
where plans for a Costa Rican trip are discussed so keep your U.S.
Passport on your body when Guerrillas or Cancer make you succumb
before living out that one full year & that random night oakwood bar asks you—
Para Donde Vas after nightlong terror-dreams of vehicular homicide & accidental
   beatings
where cocktail glassware is smashed to shards finer than Midwest snow across
   your face & neck
—though you are in the South—
where dying Englishmen buy the drinks & talk travel & give you newfound fear
   of dying
prior to living to what you perceive to be the fullest of moons within one year.

Dennis Formento

Fish in a Raincoat

For Sarah Beth Wildflower, in memory

A fish in a raincoat—
I have felt this pain all of my life.
I got this white hair by scrolling forward
slowly through time—

here with St. Anthony is a monk
with a typewriter, a man with a face full of nails, a goose
with the mouth of a snake
a heron in flight with the body of a ship

and behind it all
a village in flames, while a poor angel
all alone, flies toward the fire
with a wooden ladder.

Up, in the corner of the landscape
babies fall out of the sky

and I've got road noise in my hair
too much fine print in my life already
trailing like dust over the poor clouds

Ginger Lilies

for Maxine

I want a blade with an agenda,
a shiny glint or metallic expanse,
sharp, precise and meaningfully serrated
to sever these stalks
momentarily stopped by four nights of frost—
the ones you gave me to plant in the last millennium
a favorite of yours originating
from an Asian jungle where Bengal tigers
and black leopards paced and stalked
amid pendulous shadows
and shrill screeches of Rhesus monkeys.
You promised the lilies would grow into something
beyond fragmentary
spreading like some small-town scandal.
Eventually they took over, dominant
as one side of the brain—
both variegated and solid
topped with dense clusters of blossoms—
their pungent aroma adding spice to the bland wind,
reeds rising to an elevation above flood lines
in this city of our birth.

Malaika Favorite

A Hardback Woman

Is a serial novel
Her story never ends
Told and retold to every generation
Of her, herself and her own

A symphony of bad dreams
A book with many pages
Written in the language of now
Each day a new reality art form

She sits on the step
Watching the traffic
She has been everywhere
There is nowhere else to go

Inside her own territory
Where she planted her past
Digging in the slush pile of doubts
She is wading in liquid dreams

Fictions she told herself at nineteen
Short stories falling from her culture tree
Poems tacked to the brushstrokes
Of her painted lies

You know me
You saw me a million mirrors ago
Washing myself
When my back became a book

Published in the mud drenched river
Of old-time hurts pricked with niggles
Stitched together in the recollections
Of my many deaths

Died when I was Momma
Died when I was Sister to sister
Died when I carried brother
Died when I married lies

Dead now but rising
In the self-same memory
Typed on my back and anchored
Like a sack of beans

Each bean a word looking for dirt
To plant me and regrow
My garden of songs
Blues hurting — jazz swaying

Brett Evans

Green Ghost

Edie edits
A Basic History of the United States
in the form of Ruby
while I pick up
the aftermath of the party

I put everything we did
on a postcard and mailed it
to your old
Stuyvesant
address

it was
love, ruins
dogs, your favorite
team, & one nasty intersection
on Esplanade & Grande Route

St. John, which Julie
amplified
into a treatise
on L.A.-on- LA
violence

Bless

Mortgage

This house that we built is lovely
Here, I sleep next to you every night

Remember when we were unfamiliar. I had a plump life
you had a plump life

we were busy with our things
we tried to be loved by other people

Remember that messy life

*

But then, as they say, we got together
we had sex everyday

Who knew when I would ask the wrong question
The instant you would turn dull

But you weren't scared of scrambled eggs
You were keen to walk the dog

And now here we are every night

*

It's after midnight, sapped from balancing plates, people all night for cash
Exhausted from nailing floorboards and keeping hair off the tub

My calves ache and I don't want to give
It's the end of the month is there enough for the mortgage

I want to buy a hardback atlas, the book that split
the Germanys, took me to the USSR

pressed my kindergarten watercolors proved
my humble town existed

The atlas is $80
But we need toothpaste
I want to see a movie—can't, can't, there's not enough
it's the end of the month

I move away from you. Find your own dinner.
Do you want something or are you just hugging me good night?

*

The 1st comes—we pay the mortgage, another month
You reach out again. Your hand says Come here
All weighty words fall second to the comfort we create
I don't wonder what you want. I quickly kiss you hard.

Michael Tod Edgerton

What Yet Aureate in the Dimming

If the light if the air if March is not
enough— March or April in New Orleans
(once home, streets resonant),

one busker on Bourbon
belting Puccini arias a cappella,
In this hour of dolor, why, why, oh, Lord...,

another on Chartres,
a sultry Sam Cooke with guitar,
Then I go to my brother and I say, brother...please,

the conquistador colors
of the French Quarter
crawling toward the river,

the vining iron twisting onto
this strip of Dumaine
all yours just now (it's not enough),

no gaudy tourists jangling around,
no cameras, just your senses
breathing out to bring in

what expands your chest,
what trills your skin—
it's as if people still lived

in the Quarter (or are we
in the New World
definitively too late)—

can we still gather our selves
into another life altogether;
could we take our count differently than

opportunities and opposition, the
benched and the barred, those charged
with speech and those

sentenced to ill
legibility; could we translate
our morphologies

into a thousand new forms,
survey the world otherwise than
      Man [sic] and His
        mirror-matter;

will our hands relinquish
white-knuckled might, unknot
hawker and hooked, that we
all

might live; might the hot points
that line up to circle
their necks cool elsewise than down

to diamond chokers (*breathe*)
and the choked-off (*I
can't breathe*, he says,

he says again
and again—hear him
across centuries);

if the possibility itself
will not suffice,
its shadow leaves us

insanguine as an Idea
of thought (how could it,
how could it be

different)—then what? What
will what
world what *we*

what can we
will we
make take shape?

Jeanne Duplantier

Tending The Garden

I can not excuse myself from the garden today.
Like my spirit, it needs care.
Insects creeping about pell mell,
caterpillars, stemma guiding them
to lush foliage.
Okra flowers open with exalted allure
as does my heart when I linger,
patiently mending it.
I will not diminish the capacity
of the tomatoes, or my bruised being.
We rise up each day with encouragement
from the cucumbers, eggplants
prayer and rumination.
We mulch the soil that reinforces our feet,
scattering our herbs,
and showering the world.

King Snake

When i was young there were snakes,
    and then there were snakes.
Mark, my best friend, and i, fearless,
    trudged through
neighboring fields of thistle and cat tails
    wondering if we'd spot
any of the ones we'd pored over
    in the illustrated encyclopedias
my mom bought for me with
    Green Stamps.
"Red and yellow kill a fellow,
    Red and black friendly jack."

My dad killed a cottonmouth
    once, one that slithered
right into our backyard,
    our three rat terriers
sounding an alarm we knew wasn't
    just a stray dog or cat
crossing property lines.

Dad explained to us how you
    could tell it was poisonous,
how you could tell it wasn't
    just a plain old water snake.

Of course i already knew this
    from the illustrated encyclopedias mom
brought home for me, but i
    never quite figured out
how anyone was supposed to get

close enough to
see the pits around the snake's
        eyes, or coax it into
opening its mouth.

Besides, Mark and i knew that
        at best we'd stumble upon
a shy coral snake if we
        were lucky, but
all we ever saw was the occasional
        king snake,
some assorted rat or garter
        snakes, and even a couple i
never could find in
        the illustrated encyclopedias
mom bought with her
        Green Stamps.

At some point, of course, we stop
        looking at things that
once fascinated us,
stop trying
to identify the markings on things
        that slither by.

We realize there is little difference
        between things anyway,
that most things have the
        capacity to kill us
if we let them get close
        enough.

After Hurricane Gustav, while helping
        my dad pile debris curbside,
i saw Mark for the first time in years.
        He had come to check on his
late parents' property that his niece
        now owned, and he wandered over
to check on my dad, on his property.
        We talked about the things that
men who once poked around for snakes

together do; that is,
talked about the hurricane,
         about how lucky we all were.

i never mentioned of course that in
         my forty-first year i would die
from snake bite, venomous
         or not.

Cooley, Peter

Writing About the Stars Under My Feet

I'm singing to the blue jay in my yard
who never sang to me but will today

if I feather him a new blue enough—

Listen, he's playing the "Hallelujah Chorus"
from THE MESSIAH, assigned me a part.

Before I leave, for one of the upper branches
in the unseen, just let me question

what kind of God comes to me every day
in forms I never see till I raise wings

from the unknowns I'm lifting here, right now.

Christ-of-this- moment, Christ-of-I- hope- the- next,
what difference is there between I and me,

Christ-in-us to sing, shouting out the new man
I am, the blue jay's promise, invisible.

Trash

On the Mississippi river levee styrofoam cup in my hand

that will disintegrate in 1,000 years   I drink my coffee   stand in gravel

   in my church skirt   black velvet I wore to my mother's funeral

eleven days ago   Take a photo

    of my own shadow on the railroad tracks to Snapchat

to my daughters   while this river outside

my parents' house is risen higher than in years

                spillways opened   live oaks sunk in mud   grass

littered with plastic bags and beer cans   *Levee trash: a photo essay,*

my former self might think   that self so well versed in irony

                that careful daughter   who would take notes

on weeds and garbage and shut her notebook   now on the levee

            a white truck speeds by too fast

maybe a man who picks up shifts on rigs for extra money

            and in a former life I'd write a poem

about how that man might be dangerous

                to my daughters   now I write

       nothing

I am here to walk off my restless

                         sadness   to walk off my mother's voice

years ago after the storm when the city flooded   telling me she will never

leave New Orleans   no matter

how high water rises or how many times levees breach   telling me

         she will die in her house

         no evacuations   no hospitals

Now I know grief has its own topography   mine is

           this city and this coast

Dodd Clifton

So You Want To Be a Poet

a brave voice above the chaos
searching for the next clever line
polished in this gypsy craft,
a ruse for your own mind
with a touch of magic,
sweet imagination madness,
dark pearls dropped
to eager barfly ears,
your whole life
captured in a hollow haiku
while you're on your knees
picking up the pieces
of your broken sonnets,
all that blood on the page
in the name of art and
for that patchouli girl,
the wispy blonde with vamp eyes
who has your heart in a vise
so cheers, Mate,
the vine turning out words
rewarded by the Muse
if you're lucky enough,
but the last laughs on you,
Ulysses sailing away
on a sea of dancing light,
a shattered silver mirror
offering up all the shiny
pieces of your soul

Chris Champagne

Just Another Day In Portland

E, had shortened her name to save the Earth.
Portland was pulling a muscle trying to
stay wierdy.
E, had moved from the other America
the unwoke jurisdictions.
She was in Portland when the Ceruleans were born
A music
Based on Caucasianess.
A time before the answer to peace was assaulting a building
like the Big Bad Wolf, blowing out candles by masturbating with catchy sushi
    eating slogans.

It was depressing but there were depression leagues in Portland.
The Hippie redux on Hawthorne Avenue
needed medical attention.
only antidote was to listen to Dean Martin records while in a tanning bed.
Had to heard on vinyl to work.
Created enough angst that you could buy white guilt by the pound at Trader Joes.
But what to do with it.

E was proud of her new hometown
Loved to take visitors down to Mississippi Avenue
To food it.
This is where the fusion spots smushed bird seed, plantains, grits, and ostrich
    into lunch.
or
Take a brisket and smash peas and spinach and pita bread into
the face of an unsuspecting Christian.
Picasso pancake they coined it.

E's religion based on a deity who was a Salmon
was prevalent among her peers.
They weren't sure why but they knew in the college mind bones
that the fish was superior to, say, Episcopalians , in a dietary sense.

The tickle they got for mispronouncing Dietary Deity, put gooseflesh
on Vegans and this pleased 79% of America in secret polls
Don't tell anyone.
It was of course a mob driven madness
But it was a nicely dressed gaggle of liberal arts credits in its bloodstream.

The rain would come
They would put the customized dreamcatcher, they got online from Armenia,
    over their head and the flavor packets
Inserted into the native symbols
would create a nice herbal tea
that made them feel better
inside when they would ski their New York Times brain folds.

Yet there were hiccups even in cheap Nirvanas
ask any Buddhist in tennis shoes.
A joke about a cannibal restaurant in Papua New Guinea
led to a financial planner being banished to Tennessee.
Which was named the ad hoc Burnside Bridge death penalty.

Ingesting was a biologic imperative
No one could devise a way to eat a Douglas Fir or a way to have someone else
    eat for you at Burgerville.
Not that they didn't try.
The promise of tree eating was to pass fine miniature furniture
But even among the progressive locapure
Fantasy could not trump, science,
Bridge players were banned in the city limits
Because?
You figure it out.

Fun was reprieved in The Pearl District.
The introduction of a tilapia that could live and breed in coffee
became as synonymous with Portland as the lobster with Maine.

The horror of the invention of a cheese made from artificial creamer
almost melted Mt Hood
And the rumor of the verbal contact of humans with vegetables
Sent every Vegan to the Canadian embassy seeking asylum.
The crazy houses were full before the semantics were straightened out.
E knew that one day things would spiral out of control
She could feel it in her Midwestern capillaries.
the ones with gingham curtains blowing in a breeze.
It waltzes at first then it picked up steam in a Lindy Hop
as it Boogalooed down Sellwood.
The locavores got into a squabble about the radius of the true.
Ended up in a shooting war between New Zealand and Sweden
with ammunition made out of berries
The quick could eat the bullets before they harmed.

Street protests continued as everyone tried to accommodate
the destruction of every more they had learned on Sesame Street

Wolves all knew never to eat a Portlander
They had poisoned themselves with good intentions.
Even the boutique beers industry lost its mind.
Beer made from boiling your grandparents stuff and making bouillon cubes
Became a rage.
The word rage was banned.

Every night as Portland burned the Marxist torch
Even E in her poetic pose
Felt as if something was wrong

Things started going south as they used to say
When the animal activists crowd demanded exercise regimens for Geoducks
The muscles developed had commuters attaching buffed up mollusks onto
    light rail and riding into town for free
like hobo remoras.
A man took a whizz in a reservoir on YouTube and water was declared meat by
    the city council
The Trailblazers drafted a jockey in the first round because always taking tall
    guys was seen as discriminatory,
A sage suggested that everything was discriminatory to someone even the
    attitude of carnivorous satyr angelwing butterflies

Nervous breakdowns became so epidemic after a special new dog breed
The Portland Pitbull, bred to be nice
Started jumping off the Burnside Bridge in what
scientists later called a protest sponsored by Nature.

The afflicted humans were so proliferate that they could be seen from space by
    astronauts
Spelling out words like, Compost.

Smoking flyers handed out by activist turned out be a helluva hallucinogen and
    flights into Jamaica from PDX were banned by the Jamaican government
The Earth seemed to be rocking off its axis
Rwandan expatriates were killing people on the street for their ivory.
So out of whack were things that at daily moment of silence for world hunger
    mimes were required to scream for a whole minute due to union rules
Finally, a Gay -Navajo-Marsupial-Martian-Ewok was voted Mayor of Portland.
A deep breath was taken by a larch.
The sun came up the next day
And Portlanders found they had nothing new to protest.,
So, they just protested themselves over and over
Until small planets like objects formed around every individual within 8 miles
    of I -5
Soon everyone with a 503 area code
Had become their own galaxy.

E, her most excellent version of humanity
Took stock at Powell's.
Where conspiracy literature now took up 96 shelves
And basked in her Blue Stateness
And somewhere in Louisiana
A guy
Just a guy.
Stained his blue jeans
By dripping some duck gravy,
It was very hard to make the Earth hate Portland.
But....

Megan Burns

Raw Towns

For Bill Lavender

In the heart of deep hearts, no voodoo dolls

The shape of days, the hours we met and disappear, time

So fast it takes your breath away, how you can build a city

But still be a stranger in it, the way a story of a man floating in flood

Waters in a plastic pool will image carve into the crenellations

We call recollected history, in one lifetime you will have conversations

Barely recalled and words that turn swiftly the whole course & we

Gather here, patchwork defense mirroring, look i have unthreaded

The straight and narrow paths of arrival and departure: I would bet

Infinity in symbolic play, the truth of how any art meets and stabilizes

The future namings, you were the only person who dared say it

That maybe it was worth it to abandon the safe measures of prescriptions

That kept me numbed to wanting to die, imagined the length of travel

Insanity must venture & if love is not our place than why do we come here

If love is not how we see one another, why are we paying attention

I shed every safety net designed to cage in a whisper of what

Could your mind be missing, to be set apart from self possession

Campbell says, is the point of participation in a festival, the ritual

Of disassociation masks so fine, and even in the knowing that

We wear it, we revel in the apparition of this mythic state

This state of how we crumble from fearsome field to invulnerable

Abandoned structures, the shape of belief trembled along the loose

Sounds unspoken for in any quantum reality, once there is

there is no undoing, the error of our lives was never

Sleep's frail hold or survival in the margins, it was

Never seeing clearly how deeply the coding we designed seeped

The barycenter pulls the eye to a centered light but the burning

Of that bright, unequivocal eye is as gentle as the sound of breathing

Not to go gently, but that we do not go is the line's off course entry

Jackie Bullock

Smoke

You carried death in your chest like an elegant bird,
Caressing the iridescent feathers with plumes of smoke.
Within your body it preened and stretched,
Shaking its ruffled wings, nestling ever nearer your heart.
What began as a hummingbird, a sparrow, a goldfinch,
Grew in shape and wingspan,
Evolving and morphing through the years
Into a raven, a hawk, a vulture.

From your lungs I hear the bird's low whistle,
A wheezing call to the flock ahead.
The sound, dark and rasping, growing paler as it reaches your lips.
Those straining lips, once lush and full, glistening like carnelian,
Now resemble a thin, twisted beak.

Unseen, the bird moves, weaving a rancid nest.
Methodically, it tugs at the weft,
Tightening the slippery strands, all stained a tobacco brown.
Three oval pearls are sealed within the damp webbing,
And curled in the shimmering orbs
The fledglings lie in wait: red scaled, hollow boned,
Curved talons poised, their huge lidless eyes staring,
Ready to split their shells.

Hard Rain

for Amédé Ardoin

I don't know why weather never got into my songs. I knew hard rain,
knew how lightning strikes walkers, sheep & horses shivering in place
under trees in open pastures, hard rain leaving me for dead in the lane
half in & half out of the ditch after they ran over me, know bloody lace

& mush they had in mind for me, two men going for my head & throat,
holy receptacle of songs, going for immigrant & orphan in that only land
I knew myself in. I can talk like that now, speak several tongues in this boat

& underground drift. I am my own current in an unmarked site in red sand
next to another river. Look at maps. Rivers run next to other rivers, no note
works alone in any tune. But, back to hard rain. They left me with my hand

almost untouched, both of them clean & pretty as they'd ever been. Brain,
another matter. I was always without, without Mazie & Joulene, no grace
as I wanted grace. I stood on one leg in rice fields, blue heron, dark crane.
Look at the image I left behind. Hard rain is already written on my face.

Joseph Bienvenu

Halloween Poem

for Thaddeus Conti

Scooped and scooted
scumbling tangerine pentagrams
Double back to perdido
Root out lost vehicles strangled in seersucker

The age of aquarius disemboweled itself on the rocks
now infrared fish throb neurotoxin
Paisley salad of macho ferns
defenestrating a red chaos of melanin

That hole in the back of your shirt
you can't see don't know it's there

Olive slash of torso
won't you ease my troubled mind
in the blue-black ink of panthers
devouring calf muscles

Thick blood of dead grapes
red feline wine

All hail this drink of choice
for planetary apes who flick drops of ginger beer
at the window panes of filthy rich families

If la ventana let in the wind to vent
our unloved casements to the air

Camouflage of exposed ass cheeks
still recorded by the intermittent lens

of the brain's chameleonic ethos
kissed by the chemical light of the silver moon

I sing along to the birds who sing along to the car alarms
we yell in glitchy facsimiles of air hooting through pneumatic tubes
in fractured communion with the continent's molten core.

I know that there are no dead
only drowned men recently freed
eyelid coins tossed in the celestial fountain.

From the shoulder of the lion, I hear your claws fracture the sky's tomb.
your soul a cathode melting the sun,
a beggar echoing novenas that used to ring
in the dried up beds of holy rivers.

Grace Bauer

All My Dead Say Grace

They are milling about a spacious lawn,
waiting for the food I'm cooking over an open fire.
The pot is huge and black and bubbling wildly.
If I could breathe in this dream, I'm sure
whatever I'm stirring would stink.

But my dead look like they're having the time
of their lives. Some who died as strangers
are laughing together like the friends
they might have become. Couples are dancing
to music only they can hear, while a few wallflowers
who have planted themselves on the periphery
scan the sky for a distraction of birds.

The least I can do is make this meal
a good one, bring my bounty to the long table—
which appears now against a wall of arbor vitae,
already laid out with bone china, fine silver,
crystal glasses ready to be raised.

My dead take their seats, join hands,
bow their heads, and whisper a word
that happens to be my name, which—
if said before eating—means thanks.
Which is what I am trying to say to all my dead.

Now locally known and pronounced Dauphin (Daw' fn) Island, 'Ile Dauphine' is in the Gulf of Mexico near the Alabama coast. In 1699 the French-Canadian explorer Pierre Le Moyne d'Iberville named the island for the many human skeletons he found on its beaches. In 1708 Iberville's brother Jean-Baptiste Le Moyne de Bienville changed the name in an effort to console the young dauphine who, in France, was mourning the death of her mother.

Dolphin Island

The first to mark this shore with French leather,
his gold compass eye finds bones banked in sand.
He spits, returns to the skiff. Ile du Massacre.

Iberville two years dead, his younger brother
renames the island. Un geste politique.
The dauphine continues to grieve for her mother.

*

The summer that x-rays found shadows
swimming in my mother's lung, I stayed here,
at her father's house, in a place I mistook
to be named after dolphins, a haven from sharks.
No bones remained in the sand, just trash
and bleached ship boards, things I still see
strewn beyond the three of us as we wandered out
where the salt heat was hard to look through.

*

Grandpa's a small man. He waves his cigar.
James, the black giant who stinks of storage and port,
is clowning before him. Grandpa shows fists,
then starts to shout right! and throws dollars
for each of the heavyweight champs that we name.
One of his biceps can dance like an egg.

James' wine-yellowed eyes seem to reckon my winnings
and how he might have them. Nights he dreams sharks
at his cot, acts twice shrewd when I pay him
to give me his chore dragging in crab traps.
He'll never know the charm isn't his:
I've seen dolphins passing these breakers.

Other days crest into afternoon.
Three minds awash and nothing to say.
Grandpa's the lord in scenes James rehearses.
I think about wrecks, beasts, and beasts' play.

*

Today we dragged the traps in at sunset
near dolphins rolling down the shoreline.
Our son cried sharks! He wouldn't believe
what I told him. Not even at our bonfire
until I drank wine and mixed facts with myths
about dolphins and whale talk. His eyes leaped
at the waves when I described the shark's brain
but the word bottle-nose made him smile again.

The island's other names remained buried.
Acquisition, slaughter, the bereft dauphine,
they're tales for different seasons; for tonight
we've had pleasure, years make it clear:
crabs' claws, the weather band, stars.
Radio Mystery Theatre in darkness,
then baseball from Texas and cards
with cracked faces in sepia light.

*

My shadow on the screens of our rented cottage
now reflects the depth of this moonless night
before I give it back in watery toasts
in the names of slaves and dead kin.
Nothing left but to re-cover the children,
then come to sleep at their mother's breast.
I clasp her bones as the Gulf crashes.
Creatures, leaving voices, circle our beds.

Joan Baraskova

Docking in New York Harbor, 1908

Each step up from steerage brings her closer
to the lights of a city she could not have dreamed of.
Elizabeth Goldberg grasps her black wool skirt
by the hem, her other hand on the cold stair rail.
Her best muslin blouse sticks to her skin.
The small wooden trunk of her belongings is below.
The engines of the SS Rijndam groan to silence.

Elizabeth is young, healthy, strong.
She knows how to sew dresses and do fine embroidery.
Her needles, thimbles, and her pincushion
with its china lady on top, gift from her cousins,
are wrapped in muslin and batting in the trunk.
She cannot speak the language of the soldiers
and doctors who will send her back or let her stay.

The crowd on the deck stinks of wet wool and sweat.
The babies are dirty and sick; there has been no fresh milk.
The women yell at the children and the husbands.
No one has slept since the Rijndam left Rotterdam.
Elizabeth fears the men; they pinch and grab.
She stands in the back gulping clean night air.

In her coat pocket is a letter for her mother, Gitel.
How can she post it?
In the letter that will never reach Dubinki
Elizabeth tells Gitel about her nineteen days at sea,
how the ship rocked and the people groaned and cursed.
She has already seen things her mother will never see.
She will never see her mother again.

My grandmother tips her face up.
Her spectacles catch the stars, dimmer here
than in all of Lithuania, dimmer, dimmer,
but a few stars have followed her to America.

Stacey Balkun

Benediction
at the corner of Bayou & Broad

Blessed is the crab snagged in the trap
     for the smell of a chicken thigh

Blessed is the deck of cards, the pull of a hermit, two lovers, a fool and

Blessed is crawfish on Fridays, on Saturdays
     Sundays when the boys take to the dome all in white

Blessed is the bartender, Al, who walks his dog
     past my house but will never pick herbs without asking
          waiting instead for me to insist

               For he will use them on Taco Wednesday
               For he will keep my extra sweater on a hook behind the counter
               For he will cook us dinner on Thanksgiving

               and he will pour me a shot of whiskey
               when I tell him the good news
                    two when it's bad
                         and when I've left my husband

and I'm dating again, Al says to bring any new folks by
so he may pass judgment but

Blessed is my foolish sense for trouble and so
Blessed is the one who should have dressed better
the one who wouldn't pick up the check
the one who wanted to suck my toes

and the neighbors
and the neighborhood trees
and the neighbor with a peach tree who said
next year, baby, pick as many as you'd like

and blessed is the wide water, Mississippi, a name that drips
with disappointment, its slow rush
to meet the salty gulf   lord

bless our muddy past
bless the future
also muddy   and all of us who swim in it

Lord keep our toes from touching the murky bottom
and bless the creatures who wander the bottom, small but adorned with claws
that pinch
and how we peel back their tails, sucking our own fingers burned pink

and bless the hermit crabs that house themselves in trash
Bless them
Bless all of us who have lost
who have outgrown

Bless the search for some new love to crawl into
to call home

Dionne Charlet Baker

Magnolia

A chain of white and tan and cream suspends
resplendent in diadems to rival any temple.
Dew mars a fleur-de-lys of seamed and torn and broken
petals trampled into parchment within slivers of leaves
over silt comported Southward toward that river mouth
set aside for a City perchance by Hestia
to nurture the fragrance within the beauty of decay.
Herod could not order such a fall of magnolia
pristine and scented of purpose
descended from the branch where divide is life.
Orthanc is a trunk within a ring of such chains
idyllic in anonymity as only seeded in New Orleans.

Anne Babson

The City With Ghosts

"They want to increase tourism by filling the city with ghosts."
—Maurice Carlos Ruffin

Ignoring doctors' warnings, businessmen make big boasts.
To increase tourism, they fill the city with ghosts.

The slave market then is now our finest hotel.
Visit its bar. Sazeracs swill the city with ghosts.

First a roustabout, then a rough neck, he came upstream
For grunt work after they oil-spilled the city with ghosts.

Gothic novels stack behind every shutter. We don't
Bury the dead—no room. Books thrill the city with ghosts.

A runaway from Podunk, she hitched rides, blew truckers.
She thought she would make her way—until the city with ghosts.

We lurk behind curtains. Some of us catch new lovers.
 Perfect strangers Netflix-and-chill the city with ghosts.

"Can't you see that there is nothing to see here? You have
Imagined all the deaths!" They shill the city with ghosts.

After Katrina, moving to Beaumont, they both tried
To forget. Their thoughts wander still the city with ghosts

"Death is expensive, Miss Stella!" Shouted the tourists.
Their conference canceled, they bill the city with ghosts.

We dance away from funerals, for the dead abide
Here always. Our last rites instill the city with ghosts.

The ones who want parades now say heat kills the virus,
But July ferments and grills the city with ghosts.

Babsons survive plagues, and thus will I. I kill some rats.
I kill roaches. No one can kill the city with ghosts.

Ralph Adamo

One More Summer Shower
for Rette

Fathers go early

People vanish
There may be a stone
Or a pot of ash
Or maybe just nothing—the air, the sky
I will vanish
I don't like this
I know it is required
The other side of being alive
Tasting the world
Holding the hand
Hugging the body
Joining it even
I don't like leaving this half of things
Too much unfinished
Not begun
Left in the mind
Where it did no good at all

There might be a pot of ashes
Your friends might stumble to the river
Flop through mud and grit and drop
The ashes
So the river takes them
The river that doesn't need any more ash
Any more fathers
Or sons
That has its own life both sides of one
People vanish

You want to keep the image clear
But the image does not want clarity
Or cannot right itself
Which is just as well
As people vanish
Fathers often first
As it happens
The taste of river water
The breeze that rolls on the river's belly
The stone that it will gather
One of these days

CONTRIBUTORS

RALPH ADAMO has taught at Xavier University since 2007. He has published eight books of poetry (with a ninth ready to go), including two in the first group from Lost Roads Publishers in the late '70s. In 2002, his selected poems, *Waterblind*, was published and he won a National Endowment for the Arts fellowship in poetry the following year. In 2014 he published *Ever: Poems 2000-2014* and in 2020 *All the Good Hiding Places*. Adamo has edited *Barataria Review*, *The New Orleans Review* and currently edits both *Xavier Review* and Xavier Review Press.

ANNE BABSON's latest collection *The Bunker Book* is set in New Orleans in a time of political upheaval. Her previous collections *Messiah*, *Polite Occasions*, and *The White Trash Pantheon* are focused on other elements of the American Experience. Her work has appeared in journals on five continents. She is the author of the libretto for Lotus Lives, an opera performed in New York, Boston, and Montreal, soon to be released to video. She lives in New Orleans and teaches at Southeastern Louisiana University.

DIONNE CHARLET BAKER is a poet and freelance writer. Surviving the sudden loss of her husband, diagnosed with a benign brain tumor and dysautonomia, she writes. Her interviews, book reviews, music and entertainment articles appear in *Where Y'at Magazine*. Her poetry has been published in *Ladowich Magazine*, the *By Gaslight* Anthology Series, and the *Inklings: Louisiana Writers* Anthology Series.

STACEY BALKUN is the author of *Sweetbitter* & co-editor of *Fiolet & Wing: An Anthology of Domestic Fabulist Poetry*. Winner of the 2019 New South Writing Contest as well as Terrain.org's 10th Annual Contest, her work has appeared in *Best New Poets 2018*, *Mississippi Review*, *Pleiades*, & several other anthologies & journals. Stacey holds an MFA from Fresno State and teaches creative writing online at The Poetry Barn. She is the Coordinator for Graduate & Undergraduate English programs at the University of New Orleans.

JOAN BARASOVSKA lives in Orange County, North Carolina. She co-hosted a poetry series at the independent bookstore Flyleaf Books in Chapel Hill and serves on the Board of the North Carolina Poetry Society. In 2020 Joan was nominated for Best of the Net and a Pushcart Prize. Joan is the author of *Birthing Age* (Finishing Line Press), *Carrying Clare* (Main Street Rag), and the forthcoming collection *Orange Tulips* (Redhawk Publications).

RANDY BATES writes poetry, nonfiction, and fiction. He recently unretired to teach again in the MFA Creative Writing Workshop at UNO.

GRACE BAUER has published six collections of poems—most recently, *Unholy Heart: New and Selected Poems* (University of Nebraska/Backwaters Press, 2021). Other recent collections include *MEAN/TIME* and a 20th anniversary re-issue of *The Women At the Well*. She also co-edited the anthology *Nasty Women Poets: An Unapologetic Anthology of Subversive Verse*. Her poems, essays, and stories have appeared in numerous anthologies and journals.

JOSEPH BIENVENU, author of *Atom Parlor, Cocktail Poems*, and *Cottonmouth Incarnate*, is a poet, graphic designer, translator, and educator. A New Orleans native, Joseph spends at least half the time eating or cooking, starts working on their Mardi Gras costume six months in advance, and would rather bike around the city on a fixie than drive. Joseph is also currently in the process of translating Italian poet Vittorio Reta's poems into English. Visit josephbienvenu.com to find out more about their work.

DARRELL BOURQUE is a former Louisiana Poet Laureate, recipient of a Writer Award from the Louisiana Book Festival and a Louisiana Endowment for the Humanities Humanist of the Year Award. His newest work, *Until We Talk*, is forthcoming from Etruscan Press in Fall 2023.

JACKIE BULLOCK is from Abbeville, La. but has lived in New Orleans for over 44 years. She taught English literature at De La Salle High School, worked as a writing teacher for public schools through a program at the Contemporary Arts Center, was the program director and volunteer coordinator at WRBH 88.3 FM, the New Orleans reading radio station for the blind, and now tells stories while leading visitors through the Garden District as a tour guide.

MEGAN BURNS is the publisher at Trembling Pillow Press. She's co-hosted and hosted numerous poetry series in town including 17 Poets! Literary Series (2002-2012) and the Blood Jet Poetry Reading Series (2013-2019). Burns also founded The Dragonfly performance space and co-founded The New Orleans Poetry Festival. Her poetry publications include *Jacket Magazine, Callaloo*, and the *New Laurel Review*. She has five poetry collections including *PLURALITY* forthcoming for publication in 2023.

CHRIS CHAMPAGNE is the author of four books, including the poetry book *Roach Opera* (Portals Press, 2007) and *The Yat Dictionary* (Lavender Ink, 2013), a book on the dialect spoken by native Orleanians. A lifelong resident of New Orleans, Chris is a writer, performer, poet, comedian, political satirist, radio show host and columnist who has performed his work on stages all over the Greater New Orleans area.

DODD CLIFTON is a retired near coastal Gulf Captain, now watching great waters from the Fly and pursuing the gypsy craft of telling lyrical tales.

NICOLE COOLEY grew up in New Orleans. She is the author of several poetry collections, chapbooks and a novel. *Girl after Girl* (Louisiana State Press 2017) and *Of Marriage* (Alice James Books 2018) are her most recent books. Her awards include The Walt Whitman Award from the Academy of American Poets, a Discovery/The Nation Award, an NEA, a Creative Artists fellowship from the American Antiquarian Society, and the Emily Dickinson Award from the Poetry Society of America. Currently, she is director of the MFA Program in Creative Writing and Literary Translation at Queens College-City University where she is a professor of English.

PETER COOLEY is a native of the Midwest and graduate of Shimer College, the University of Chicago and the Writers Workshop at the University of Iowa. He has lived over half of his life in New Orleans where he was Professor of English and Director of Creative Writing at Tulane University from 1975-2018. He has published eleven books of poetry, ten of them with Carnegie Mellon and his work has appeared in *The New Yorker, The Atlantic, The Nation, The New Republic* and over one hundred anthologies. Cooley was Poetry Editor of *North American Review* from 1970-2000 and is currently Poetry Editor of *Christianity and Literature*. He is Professor Emeritus at Tulane University and former Louisiana Poet Laureate.

TOBY DASPIT is Professor of Education and Department Head of Educational Curriculum and Instruction at the University of Louisiana at Lafayette. He serves as Emeritus Consultant for the National Writing Project of Acadiana and is the author of the chapbooks *Bar Coasters* (Yellow Flag Press) and *Anatomy of a Ghost and other poems not about you* (Southern Hum Press). Toby is finalizing his first full-length poetry collection, *Kintsugi*.

JEANNE DUPLANTIER was born in New Orleans and has lived here all her life. Now retired, she was a teacher in the New Orleans Public School system for thirty-four years, where she taught preschool children with special needs. She was also a teacher of adult education in the St. Thomas Housing Development in the 1980s, as well as a volunteer with hospice during the AIDs crisis. She currently sings in a hospice choir, which she describes as one of the greatest gifts of her life. Jeanne participated in the poetry buffet last August along with members of her writing group.

MICHAEL TOD EDGERTON (he/they) is a gayboy poet of lyrically fluid gender and genre alike. Author of *Vitreous Hide* (Lavender Ink), Tod's poems have appeared in *Boston Review, Denver Quarterly, EOAGH, Interim, New American Writing, Posit, Sonora Review, VOLT,* and other journals. He's received scholarships from Bread Loaf and Napa Valley writers' conferences and a MacDowell fellowship. Tod holds an MFA from Brown and a PhD from UGA. He currently teaches at San José State

University and serves on the poetry-editing team of *Seneca Review*. You'll find him swishing along the streets of San Francisco and online at mtodedge.com.

NICOLE M.K. EIDEN is a writer and baker. Her poem "Embodiment" was the 2021 Words and Music Writing Contest co-runner up. Her poem "Mortgage" appeared in the *2019 New Poetry from the Midwest* (New American Press) and won third place in the 2016 Women's National Book Association Writing Contest. Kirkus Reviews selected her debut collection, *I Am One of You* (Mississippi Sound Publishing, 2016), as a featured book in their Indie category. Originally from Ohio, Nicole co-owns Windowsill Pies, a Southern-style pie and tart company in New Orleans, where she lives with her husband and daughter.

BRETT EVANS is a native Orleanian who loves ferries, pho, and feeling fine at the Fly- - and now even the Lakefront, near his new Gentilly home. Works include *Phone-In Masterpieces*, (with Chris Shipman) *Keats is Not the Problem*, and *I Love This American Way of Life*. His is a founding member of the 'tit-Rex parade, and the band Skin Verb. See him read poems to flowers on Instagram @brettevans429.

MALAIKA FAVORITE won the 2016 Broadside Lotus Press Naomi Long Madgett Poetry Award for her collection, *Ascension*, published in 2016 by Broadside Lotus Press. Her publications include: *Dreaming At the Manor* (Finishing Line Press 2014) and *Illuminated Manuscript* (New Orleans Poetry Journal Press, 1991). Malaika recently won the Cosmographia Books prize for Spiritual Fiction. Her novel will be published in 2022.

GINA FERRARA lives and writes in New Orleans. She has published five poetry collections, including her latest, *AMISS* (Dos Madres Press 2023). Her work has appeared in *Poetry East*, *The Briar Cliff Review*, and *The Poetry Ireland Review* among others. Since 2007, she has curated The Poetry Buffet, a monthly reading series that happens the first Saturday of most months. She teaches English and writing at Delgado Community College and has work forthcoming in *The Delmarva Review*.

DENNIS FORMENTO lives in Slidell, LA, USA, near his native New Orleans. Books of poetry include *Spirit Vessels* (FootHills Publishing, 2018), *Cineplex* (Paper Press, 2014,) *Looking for An Out Place* (FootHills Publishing, 2010.) Edited *Mesechabe: The Journal of Surregionalism* 1990-2001. St. Tammany Parish organizer of poetry events for 100,000 Poets for Change, a network of poets for peace, sustainability and justice world-wide.

ELIZABETH GARCIA is now retired after having worked 21 years, some of them beautiful, some of them brutal, for the City Of New Orleans. She has a love for the ARchiTecture & a gratefulness for the consistent mystery of navigation through the City of NO due to the placement of the River. She has been published in the *Bacopa*

Literary Review, Big Bridge, New Orleans Sturm & Drang, YAWP, Spillwords Press, & *Sinister Goat Review*. Her photographs have won awards in the National Arts Program, City of New Orleans.

JOHN GERY has published seven collections of poetry, including *Davenport's Version, A Gallery of Ghosts,* and *Have at You Now!*. In 2021, his award-winning collection, *The Enemies of Leisure,* was re-issued by Red Hen Press. He has also published widely as a critic of American modernist and contemporary poetry. A Research Professor of English at the University of New Orleans, he directs the Ezra Pound Center for Literature, Brunnenburg, Italy, and is the Editor of the EPCL Book Series at Clemson University Press.

ANYA GRONER's essays, stories, and poems can be found in *The Oxford American, The Atlantic,* the *New York Times* and elsewhere. She teaches creative writing at NOCCA and was a founding member of the New Orleans Writers Workshop..

GEORGE GUIDA is author of ten books, including the recent poetry collections *Zen of Pop* (Long Sky Media, 2020) and *New York and Other Lovers* (Encircle Publications, 2020). His latest books are the novels *Posts from Suburbia* (Encircle, 2022) and *The Uniform* (Guernica Editions, 2024). He teaches writing, literature and film at New York City College of Technology and coordinates the Finger Lakes Reading and Performance Series at his family's cafe', the MacFadden Coffee Company, in Western New York.

KELLY HARRIS-DEBERRY is the author of the poetry collection, *Freedom Knows My Name*. Her work has been featured in various publications. Kelly is the recipient of fellowships from the Fine Arts Work Center and Cave Canem, and earned degrees from Kent State University and Lesley University. kellyhd.com

NANCY C. HARRIS was born in New York but has lived most of her life in New Orleans. She received her B.A. and M.A. degrees from Newcomb and Tulane University. She has organized poetry readings at the Maple Leaf Bar after the death of Everette Maddox in 1989 until the Ides of March, 2020. The reading series resumed in October of 2022.

ASHLEY MACE HAVIRD (Shreveport. LA) is the author of two poetry collections: *Wild Juice* (LSU Press, 2021) and *The Garden of the Fugitives* (Texas Review Press, 2014), which won the X. J. Kennedy Poetry Prize, and two chapbooks. Her novel, *Lightningstruck* (Mercer University Press, 2016), won the Ferrol Sams Award for Fiction. Her poems have appeared in many journals including *Shenandoah, Southern Review,* and *Image,* and in anthologies such as *Hard Lines: Rough South Poetry*. Havird was the Caddo Parish Poet Laureate from 2018-2021.

DAVID HAVIRD is the author most recently of *Weathering* (Mercer University

Press, 2020), a "chimeric omnibus" of poetry and memoir. His poems and essays have appeared in many periodicals including *Agni*, the *Hopkins Review*, *Literary Imagination*, and the *Yale Review*. A professor emeritus at Centenary College of Louisiana, he lives in Shreveport.

AVA LEAVELL HAYMON, former Poet Laureate of the State of Louisiana, is poet, playwright, editor, and teacher. Widely published, both in journals and in anthologies, her fourth full-length poetry collection, *Eldest Daughter* (LSU Press), is a life's work that grapples with a preacher's daughter upbringing. Her poems are used as text by classical and jazz composers, recently released in a CD, *Watercolors*, by Robert Nelson. She edits the Barataria Poetry Series for LSU Press.

CAROLYN HEMBREE is the author of *Skinny* and *Rigging a Chevy into a Time Machine and Other Ways to Escape a Plague*, winner of the Trio Award and the Rochelle Ratner Memorial Award. Her poems are out or forthcoming in *Beloit Poetry Journal*, *Copper Nickel*, *Poetry Daily*, *The Southern Review*, and other publications. She teaches at the University of New Orleans and serves as the poetry editor of *Bayou Magazine*.

ARDEN ELI HILL holds a Ph.D in Creative Writing from the University of Nebraska-Lincoln with a specialization in Women and Gender Studies and an MFA from Hollins University. *Willow Springs*, *Western Humanities Review*, *Kaleidoscope*, the Lambda Literary award-winning anthology *First Person Queer*, its sequel, *Second Person Queer* are among Arden's publications. Forthcoming work will appear in the anthology *Trans Bodies Trans Selves* (Tupelo Press Quarterly). Learn more about Arden at ardenelihill.com.

RAYMOND "MOOSE" JACKSON constantly pushes his poetry out of conventional spaces. His work has been applied to live environmental theater such as *Loup Garou* and *Cry You One* (Mondo Bizarro and ArtSpot Productions), rock and experimental bands like Liquid Land and Shock Patina, on the street, at festivals, in ceremonies and art installations. His latest collection of poems, *Dreaming in the Bone Boat* was published by UNO Press (2022).

SKYE JACKSON's work has appeared or is forthcoming in *The Southern Review*, *Electric Literature*, *Green Mountains Review*, *RATTLE* and elsewhere. Her chapbook *A Faster Grave* won the 2019 Antenna Prize. Her work was a finalist for the RATTLE Prize, the RHINO Founders' Prize, and in 2021 she received the AWP Intro Journals Award and was twice nominated for the Pushcart Prize and Best New Poets. Jackson's work was selected by Billy Collins for inclusion in the *Library of Congress Poetry 180 Project*. In 2022, she served as the Writer-In-Residence at the Key West Literary Seminar in Florida.

SANDRA GRACE JOHNSON lives in New Orleans.

RODGER KAMENETZ's latest book of poetry is *The Missing Jew: Poems 1976-2022* (Ben Yehuda). His other recent books of poetry are *Yonder* (Lavender Ink, 2018) and *Dream Logic* (PURH, 2020). His poems have appeared lately in the *Southern Review, New Orleans Review, Image,* and *Ayin.*

JULIE KANE is Professor Emerita at Northwestern State University in Natchitoches, currently teaching in the low-residency MFA program at Western Colorado University. She was the 2011-2013 Louisiana Poet Laureate. Her five books of poetry include *Rhythm & Booze,* winner of the National Poetry Series; *Jazz Funeral,* winner of the Donald Justice Poetry Prize; and *Mothers of Ireland,* winner of the Poetry by the Sea Book Award. With Grace Bauer, she co-edited *Nasty Women Poets: An Unapologetic Anthology of Subversive Verse.*

JASON KERZINSKI is a poet and street portrait photographer living in New Orleans.

DWAIN KITCHELL's father read *Best Loved Poems* to him as a child and Dwain has been tinkering with words ever since.

JONATHAN KLINE is a storyteller, fiction writer, visual artist, and poet. He received his MFA in storytelling form the School of the Art Institute of Chicago and has performed in New York City, Chicago, Seattle, Dublin and Cork, Ireland. He is the author of *The Wisdom of Ashes* and *Standing at the Gate* (Lavender Ink 2017 and 2022). Kline's stories have been published in *Xavier Review, The Maple Leaf Rag* and *Indigent Press,* and his poems have appeared in *Tribes Magazine, Big Bridge,* and *The Journal of American Poetry.*

JUSTIN LACOUR lives in New Orleans and edits *Trampoline: A Journal of Poetry.* His chapbook *My Heart is Shaped Like a Bed: 46 Sonnets* was recently released by Fjords Books.

BILL LAVENDER is a poet, novelist, musician, carpenter, and publisher living in New Orleans. *MY ID,* his eleventh book of poetry, was published by BlazeVox in 2019. He founded Lavender Ink, a small press devoted mainly to poetry, in 1995, and Diálogos, an imprint devoted to cross-cultural literatures (mostly in translation) in 2011. Lavender Ink/ Diálogos now have more than 200 books in print. He is also the co-founder of the New Orleans Poetry Festival.

DANIEL W.K. LEE (李華強) is a third-generation refugee, queer, Cantonese American born in Kuching, Malaysia. He earned his MFA in Creative Writing - Poetry at The New School, and his debut collection of poetry, *Anatomy of Want,* was published by QueerMojo/Rebel Satori Press in 2019. Daniel makes New Orleans his home with his head-turning whippet Camden. Find out more about him at danielwklee.com or follow him: @strongplum on Instagram / @danielsaudade on Twitter.

CAMERON LOVEJOY is the editor and publisher at Tilted House, a small press in New Orleans. His work has appeared or is forthcoming in *DIAGRAM*, *Xavier Review*, *North Dakota Quarterly*, *Poets Reading the News*, *Barrelhouse*, *Bayou*, and more.

MARTHA MCFERREN received an MFA from Warren Wilson College and is the author of six books, including *Women in Cars*, for which she received the Marianne Moore Prize, *Archaeology at Midnight* and, most recently, *The McFerren Plot*. Her poems have appeared in *Georgia Review*, *Shenandoah*, *Southern Review*, and many other journals and anthologies. She is the recipient of an Artist Fellowship in Literature by the Louisiana Arts Council, a Yaddo Fellowship and a National Endowment for the Arts Creative Writing Fellowship. A native Texan, she now lives in New Orleans with her husband, woodturner Dennis Wall.

A native of New Orleans, KAREN MACEIRA holds an MFA from Penn State. Her poems have appeared in numerous journals such as *The Beloit Poetry Journal*, *Louisiana Literature*, *The New Orleans Review*, *Xavier Review*, and *English Journal*. Her reviews have appeared in *The Harvard Review*, and her essays in the *Hollins Critic* and the *Journal of College Writing*. Her chapbook entitled *My Father and the Astros* was published in 2019.

BRENNA MAHN is an artist-poet who grew up on army bases and across several states, now based in Louisiana. She is a member of the New Orleans Queer Writing group and has had solo exhibitions with the Ohio Art League and the Lowell Art Gallery and her work published with Louisiana Words and Dialogue Magazine.

MONICA MANKIN is a poet and an Associate Professor of English at Delgado Community College in New Orleans, LA, where she has lived for over a decade. Originally from Southern California, she earned a B.A. in Creative Writing from the University of California, Riverside, and an M.F.A. in Poetry from the University of Idaho, Moscow. She recently earned a grant from Can Serrat, Spain, to attend their Writer's Residency in June 2023 where she will complete her current poetry project, *Almanac for the End of Time*. More can be found at http://moneikōn.com/.

MIKE MARINA is a local poet, chef, and all around performer. His work has been featured in the Esoterotica anthologies *Enflame* and *Hand-Bound*. He was also co-writer of the show *Beyond Desire* and was also featured in the anthology of the same name. When not performing onstage at open mics, Mike can be found hosting food pop ups at burlesque shows and other nightly events.

PATRICE MELNICK is a writer, arts administrator and arts activist. She has published a poetry chapbook, *City of Hey Baby* (Finishing Line Press.) and a memoir, *Po-boy Contraband: from Diagnosis Back to Life* (Catalyst Press). Melnick is director of the Opelousas Museum and Interpretive Center and lives in Grand Coteau with her loving and very patient husband, Olan Thibodeaux.

MONICA CAROL MILLER is an assistant professor of English at Middle Georgia State University in Macon, Georgia. A founding member of the New Orleans Women's Poetry Conspiracy, she is the author of *Being Ugly: Southern Women Writers and Social Rebellion* (LSU Press, 2017), co-editor of *The Tacky South* (LSU Press, 2022), and editor of *Dear Regina: Flannery O'Connor's Letters from Iowa* (UGA Press, 2022).

Z.W. MOHR lives in the very magical, and often wet, city of New Orleans, but was raised in the dry foothills above Los Angeles. Being raised on stories told by firelight, and traveling to the hidden temples of long gone civilizations at a young age, might have unlocked doors of imagination he's never learned how to close.

MARIAN D MOORE's collection of poetry, *Louisiana Midrash*, was published by UNO Press/Runagate in January 2019. Her poetry has been published in the journals *Drumvoices*, *The Louisiana Review*, *Bridges*, *Asimov's SF* magazine, the anthologies *Mending for Memory: Sewing in Louisiana Essays, Stories, and Poems*, *Dominion: An Anthology of Speculative Fiction from Africa and the African Diaspora* and *I am New Orleans…*

GAIL MORGAN grew up in a military family that moved nine times before she was fourteen. This early sense of dislocation keeps her rooted in the New Orleans community. She received a BA in fine art from Newcomb and later an MFA in performance art from Tulane. She is a visual and performance artist, teacher of art and Tai Chi, and since Katrina, a photographer of all things botanical. Her work has been shown in various galleries and performance venues.

A native of Mississippi, BENJAMIN MORRIS is a writer, researcher, and the author of one book of nonfiction and two books of poetry, most recently *Ecotone* (Antenna/Press Street Press, 2017). His work has appeared in such places as *The Oxford American* and *The Southern Review*, and received fellowships from the Mississippi Arts Commission, Tulane University, and A Studio in the Woods, as well as the 2021 Words & Music Writing Competition for Poetry. He lives in New Orleans, where he serves as one of the coordinators for the New Orleans Poetry Festival.

GEOFF MUNSTERMAN is the author of four chapbooks and one full-length collection, *Because the Stars Shine Through It* (Lavender Ink). His work has been published in Esoterotica's *Longing*, *The Raging Pelican*, *Xavier Review*, and *Fine*

Print. He currently serves as an editor/designer for Black Widow Press. He grew up in Plaquemines Parish but now lives and works on Chartres Street in New Orleans.

KAY MURPHY is Professor Emerita in English from the University of New Orleans. Since her retirement she continues to teach in the Study Abroad programs and serve on MFA theses in poetry. Her most recent publication is editor of *On A Wednesday Night*, an anthology of student and faculty poetry that celebrates twenty-five years of the Creative Writing Workshop at the University of New Orleans. She received a UNO Author Award in 2022.

AUSTIN NIELI is a poet from New Orleans and related nearby areas. He hosted the reading series "Eublablabla" from 2019-2021, and his work has appeared in *Blazing Stadium*. Chapbooks have been published by Reverse Catfish Press, False Dimensions, and his chapbook *Some Prayers* inaugurated the 24 Hour Store Chapbook Series, of which he is a co-editor. He is currently absorbed in translating *The Gaucho Martín Fierro* by José Hernández, as well as writing the longest poem he has ever written.

BILJANA D. OBRADOVIĆ is a Serbian-American poet, critic, editor, translator, and Professor of English at Xavier University of Louisiana. She has published five poetry collections including *Little Disruptions* (Word Tech Editions 2023) which was previously published only in Serbia. Her newest translations of Serbian language poet Dubraka Djuric's *The Politics of Hope (After the War): New and Selected Poems* will appear in 2023 from New York's Roof Books.

Originally from the Canadian Maritimes, ANTHONY OSCAR is a New Orleans-based poet, songwriter and visual artist. He is a longstanding member of the New Orleans Community Printshop and Darkroom where he collaborates with likeminded artists to offer accessible art-making resources to the Greater New Orleans community with a special focus on youth and underrepresented emerging artists. He has released three self-produced albums, as well as *Weird Sleep*, his first book of poems and drawings.

MELINDA PALACIO is an award-winning poet who divides her time between Santa Barbara and New Orleans. In addition to three books of poetry, she has written a novel, *Ocotillo Dreams*, and was recently named Poet Laureate of Santa Barbara.

ANDREA PANZECA grew up in Merrit Island, Florida. She is the author of two chapbooks *Rusty Baskets and Daisy Bells* and *Weird...Joe Pesci.* She earned an MFA in creative non-fiction from the University of New Orleans. Her poetry and non-fiction have appeared in *Ellipsis*. She lives in New Orleans and has taught with arts organizations including KID SmART, the Contemporary Arts Center, and Lelia Haller Ballet Classique.

LISA PASOLD is a writer originally from Montreal, now based in New Orleans. She is the author of 5 critically-acclaimed books. Lisa's 2012 poetic narrative, *Any Bright Horse*, was shortlisted for Canada's Governor General's Award. Lisa's poetry has appeared in *The Atlanta Review*, *The Los Angeles Review*, *Fence* and *New American Writing*. She takes pictures of flowers @lisapasold.

ALISON PELEGRIN is the author of four poetry collections, including *Waterlines*. She has received a fellowship from the National Endowment of the Arts as well as an ATLAS grant from the Louisiana Board of Regents. She is writer-in-residence at Southeastern Louisiana University

JONATHAN PENTON founded the electronic journal *Unlikely Stories* in 1998, and its daughter imprint Unlikely Books in 2005. He serves and has served in an editorial, management, for *Bridge*, *MadHat, Inc.*, and *Rigorous: a journal by people of color*. His own books of poems include *BACKSTORIES* (Argotist Ebooks) and *Standards of Sadiddy* (Lit Fest Press). He lives in New Orleans.

VALENTINE PIERCE is a spoken word artist, writer, editor, graphic designer. Pierce dabbles in photograph and crafts. She is a former journalist and photojournalist but these days she focuses on graphic design, including brochures, editing, proofreading, book design/layout, flyers, posters and more. She has two published books: *Geometry of the Heart* (Portals Press, 2007) and *Up Decatur* (New Laurel Review Press, 2017) and has been published in several anthologies, including *I am New Orleans*, *Nasty Women Poets*, *Cape Cod Review*, *Mending for Memory*, *New Laurel Review*, *Maple Leaf Rag*, and *Bayou Magazine*.

SARAH A. RAE is a poet and former high school educator who lives in Chicago. Recent publications include her chapbook, *Someplace Else* (dancing girl press, 2020), and poems in *On a Wednesday Night* (University of New Orleans Press, 2019). Other work appears or is forthcoming in *Naugatuck River Review*, *Burlesque Press*, *Revista Blanca Y Negro*, and *Jet Fuel Review*, among others. Her translations of work by the Mexican poet Guadalupe Ángela appear in the journal *Ezra* and are forthcoming in video format in Jill!, A Women+ In Translation Reading Series. She holds an MFA in Creative Writing from the University of New Orleans, and is a native of Champaign, Illinois.

BEVERLY RAINBOLT earned her MFA in the Creative Writing Workshop at UNO (2000) She authored a poetry collection, *The Altar of this Moment* (Portals Press, 2001) and co-edited with Kay Murphy another, *Women's Workshop Into Print*, (In-Heritance Press, 2003). She has also been published in *Quarterly West*, *Big Muddy: A Journal of the Mississippi River Valley*, *On A Wednesday Night*, *20 Pounds of Headlights*, and several issues of *Maple Leaf Rag*, *Quarterly West*.

BRAD RICHARD is the author of four poetry collections (most recently, *Parasite*

Kingdom, The Word Works, 2019 – Winner of the 2018 Tenth Gate Prize) and four chapbooks (most recently, *In Place*, 2022, Seven Kitchens Press – selected for the Robin Becker Series). He is on the faculty of the Kenyon Review Writers Workshop for Teachers and New Orleans Writers Workshop. Series editor of the Hilary Tham Capital Collection (an imprint of The Word Works), he lives, writes, edits, gardens, and occasionally teaches in New Orleans. More at bradrichard.org.

MATT ROBINSON may look like a mild-mannered poet behind a typewriter on Frenchmen Street, but he also drives a truck that could use a tune-up. He believes he's figured out the "why" of pine trees, and if Serendipity were an attribute to his D&D character, he'd have a natural 18. He would like to remind people that they always have the right to remain silent. Ever since he found out he has a peach tree growing in his yard, he has a new spring in his step. His work has not been published in years.

DENISE M. ROGERS is a teacher of literature and composition and the former Director of the Writing Center at the University of Louisiana at Lafayette. Her poems have appeared in *Alaska Quarterly Review, Louisiana Literature, WordRiver, Glass*, and other journals. Her first book, *The Scholar's Daughter*, was published through Louisiana Literature Press.

CAROLINE ROWE is a lifelong resident of the French Quarter in New Orleans. Her work has most recently appeared in *The Bangalore Review, Cathexis Northwest*, and *Blazing Stadium*. Her poetry has received nominations for the Pushcart Prize, as well as the Nancy D. Hargrove Editor's Prize from The *Jabberwock Review*. Her debut chapbook *God's Favorite Redhead* was published in 2020 by Lucky Bean Press.

DAVID ROWE's poetry has appeared in journals including the *North American Review*, the *Cortland Review, Exquisite Corpse*, & *Big Bridge*, as well as in the anthologies, *Maple Leaf Rag* (Portals Press), *The Great Sympathetic* (NAR Press), & the *Southern Poetry Anthology* (Texas Review Press). A full-length collection, *Unsolicited Poems*, was published by Verna Press, & a spoken-word album, *File Under: Poetry*, is available through Bandcamp. A native of Worcester, Mass., he lives in the Carrollton neighborhood of New Orleans with his wife, poet Caroline Rowe.

ED RUZICKA's most recent book of poems is *My Life in Cars*. Ed's poems have appeared in the *Atlanta Review, RATTLE, Canary, Xavier Review,* and many other literary publications. Ed has been a finalist for the Dana Award, the New Millennium Award and others. Ed lives with his wife, Renee, in Baton Rouge, LA. More at: edrpoet.com/poems

Author & Folklorist, Educator and Scholar, MONA LISA SALOY's work appears in many anthologies and journals. Dr. Saloy is an active Educator and Scholar who is a noted speaker and storyteller who consults to the Louisiana Endowment for the Humanities (LEH), the Louisiana Division of the ARTS (LDOA) and is an active member of the Louisiana Folklore Society. She has composed a praise song and performed for two presidents. *Black Creole Chronicles*, her latest collection of poetry, was published by UNO Press in 2023, and since 2021 she has served as Louisiana Poet Laureate.

SANDRA SARR is a poet and writer in Baton Rouge, Louisiana, with a talent for finding unwanted animals good homes. She is communications manager at LSU School of Veterinary Medicine.

MARTHA SERPAS's most recent poetry collection is *Double Effect*. She teaches creative writing at University of Houston, is a hospital chaplain, and calls Bayou Lafourche home.

CHRISTOPHER SHIPMAN (he/him) lives on Eno, Sappony & Shakori land in Greensboro, NC where he teaches literature and creative writing at New Garden Friends School. He plays drums in The Goodbye Horses. Recent work appears or is forthcoming in *Denver Quarterly*, *Iron Horse*, *Poetry Magazine* and *Rattle* (online). His experimental play *Metaphysique D'Ephemera* has been staged at four universities. *Getting Away with Everything* (Unlikely Books, 2021) a collaboration with Vincent Celluci is his most recent collection. www.cshipmanwriting.com.

SHERYL ST. GERMAIN has published six poetry books, three essay collections, and has co-edited two anthologies of essays and poems. Recently retired as Director of the MFA Creative Writing program at Chatham University in Pittsburgh, she now resides in Savannah, Georgia, where she continues to write and make art quilts inspired by both poetry and the natural world. She received the Louisiana Writer Award in 2018. Her most recent book is *Fifty Miles*, published by Etruscan Press in 2020.

SHADOW ANGELINA STARKEY is an Anishinaabe, Tslangi, Cajun poet and photographer whose family has called New Orleans home since 1727. Her photography has been featured in magazines, the New Orleans Museum of Art, the Library of Congress and numerous galleries. She has two collections of her writing: *The Heart of a Hurricane is Fear on a Sage in a Monsters Ballet* and *Barbed Choir*, both published by Next Left Press. Starkey has performed original work in The New Orleans Fringe Festival, Esoterotica (which she co-produces), and stages across the world.

PARIS TATE is the author of one poetry collection titled *All the Words in Between*. Her poetry can also be found in the anthology *Maple Leaf Rag*, as well as *Tilted House Review*, *The New Guard Review* and *Infection House*, a New Orleans-based online literary magazine that focused on the COVID-19 pandemic and other events that defined 2020. Tate lives near New Orleans, Louisiana with her husband, where she works as a librarian in a small library located in the small city of Harahan, Louisiana.

RANDOLPH THOMAS is the author of the poetry collection *The Deepest Rooms*, winner of the George Cable book award. His poems have recently appeared in *Southern Poetry Review*, *The Common*, *Poetry South*, *Pleiades*, *Poetry Daily*, and *Verse Daily*. He is also the author of the short story collection *Dispensations*, and his nonfiction has recently appeared in *Appalachian Review*. He teaches at LSU.

NIKKI UMMEL is a queer writer, editor, and educator in New Orleans. Nikki has been published or is forthcoming in *Painted Bride Quarterly*, *The Adroit*, *The Georgia Review*, and more. She has been nominated for a Pushcart Prize, Best New Poets, and twice awarded an Academy of American Poets Award. She is the 2022 winner of the Leslie McGrath Poetry Prize. Her chapbook, *Hush*, was published by Belle Point Press (2023). You can find her on the web at www.nikkiummel.com.

New Orleanian JAN VILLARUBIA is a published, award-winning poet and playwright. Her poetry collection, *Return to Bayou Lacombe* was published by Cinnamon Press in Wales. Her poetry has appeared in literary journals and anthologies including *The Literary Review*, *The Southern Poetry Anthology* and *New Laurel Review*. Her full-length published plays are *Miz Lena's Backyard* and *Odd Fellow's Rest*. She received a Theater Fellowship from the Louisiana State Arts Council and the National Endowment for the Arts. Besides enjoying her 4-year-old identical grandsons, she is currently working on a poetry collection which incorporates antique portraits of women.

ANDY YOUNG's second full-length collection, *Museum of the Soon Departed* will be published by Carnegie Mellon Press in 2024. She is also the author of *All Night It Is Morning* (Diálogos Press) and four chapbooks. Her work has recently appeared or is forthcoming in *The Southern Review*, *Pank* and *The Journal of the American Medical Association*. Her translations from the Arabic, with Khaled Hegazzi, were included in the Norton anthology *Language for a New Century*. She teaches at the New Orleans Center for Creative Arts.

RAINA ZELINSKI was raised in the verdant entropy of New Orleans where she continues to reside with her partner and child. She teaches high school at the New Orleans Center for the Creative Arts and co-manages Lucky Bean Poetry, a small press and reading series. Her first chapbook *diminution* was published in 2019. Her poetry has recently appeared in *nurture: a literary journal*, *Tilted House*, *Trampoline: A Journal of Poetry*, and *DYNAMIS*.

POSTSCRIPT

As far as I can tell, credit for the name *The New Orleans Poetry Journal* goes to *Chicago Review's* then-editor Reed Whittemore. Richard Ashman, torn between *Quicksilver* and *A Houynihm's Scrapbook*, solicited advice from the editor who had recently accepted his work and was summarily advised that people would submit to *The New Orleans Poetry Journal* simply for it having New Orleans in the name. "As for finding an audience," he added, "if you manage it, let me know how."

Launching in January of 1955, the New Orleans Poetry Journal launched with a brief preface that begins:

> One of our contributors has sent us the comment: "It is instructive to watch two people" (like the editors) "start from poetic scratch to edit a magazine. You make errors that no one else would make," and his reasons follow. Letters have tones, overtones, and direct, unambiguous statement. The overtones in this letter are such that we fear this contributor will submit no more, and we are contritely sorry. And we applaud his concern. But, having advanced, we cannot recede. The correspondent might have made us feel better by saying, "scratch, plus half a scratch."

By trade, Ashman worked as the director for cardiology [known then as the heart station] for Charity Hospital. Maxine Cassin was a recent graduate of Newcomb and Tulane working in Dr. Ashman's office. Little magazines were popping up all over America and together, Ashman and Cassin were encouraged to establish something new. Only lasting sixteen issues (with a four-issue supplement, *A Houynihm's Scrapbook*, in its final year and a quartet of chapbooks by individual poets), *The New Orleans Poetry Journal* published six future Pulitzer Prize winners, five future United States Poet Laureates, Guggenheim recipients, National Book Award Winners—all at the beginning of their illustrious tenures as standard-bearers of American arts and letters. One interesting omission is Anne Sexton, who subscribed to the *NOPJ* and corresponded with Ashman after an initial rejection. He pointed her in the direction of a few journals to also submit work to, for which she responded to a few weeks later thanking him for the assistance in receiving her first ever acceptance in a literary journal. Ashman and Cassin even accepted for publication what became known as "Unknown Girl in a Maternity Ward" but the journal folded before they were able to feature it. Sexton went on to a workshop with Robert Lowell, a Pulitzer, literary infamy rivaled only by Sylvia Plath (whose first in-print publication, unlike Sexton's, the *NOPJ* did manage to feature). In one letter during their correspondence, Sexton wrote: "Writing can be a very lonely process. You were the first editor to give me some note of encouragement...I walk the day upside down until the mail man arrives. NOPJ has such a fine reputation and is needed."

It's hard building anything from scratch. If you have capital, a name, a small handful of serious people—even then, you will fight tide. Ashman had a real job and could therefore pay poets more than the meager $2 subscription fee amounted to ($20 today). Maxine Cassin established herself as not only a gifted editor by the quality of poets selected but an excellent manager, keeping straight the financials and updating rosters of both subscribers and contributors.

Ashman passed away in 1970 and, with the exception of a few poems published in a few little magazines, his name and contribution left no visible mark. Maxine balanced the work of the *NOPJ* while working as a real estate agent in New Orleans, relaunching as a press more focused on the work of writers in the city. The first *Maple Leaf Rag* was a NOPJ title. She followed it with *The Everette Maddox Songbook*, Charles Black's *The Waking Passenger*, and Martha McFerren's *Delusions of a Popular Mind*. As McFerren said recently about Maxine: "She specialized in publishing books by people nobody else could get along with."

The NOPJ Press chugged along for more than 25 years releasing books and providing patronage to local poets until Hurricane Katrina effectively brought and end to it. From its inception until its final years, the constant was Maxine Cassin. Her editorial drive and vision, her steady and steadfast passion, kept the blood pumping. Continuing without her particular curiosity and response, her beautiful succinctness and precision.

Having advanced, we cannot recede. Starting from scratch, plus two and a half scratches, Gina Ferrara and I intend on building something from the nothing of a seventy year legacy few people acknowledge. This collection, which attempts with its existence to pay homage to the works of Gina, Maxine, and Richard Ashman (and numerous co-editors: R. G. Lowrey and John Gery, among others) while concurrently showcasing a diversity of voices featured during The Poetry Buffet's sixteen-year run, offers no real answer to the function and nature of poetry nor does it attempt to establish a particular school of thought on how "real poetry" should look and sound. Some of the poets are not New Orleanians, others have lived in New Orleans their entire lives. We ordered the poems in reverse alphabetical because poor Ralph always appears first in Louisiana anthologies and Andy Young always last or near-last. We read it like that and saw poems talking to one another, so it stuck. If this was a mistake, take instruction from it.

Printed in the USA
CPSIA information can be obtained
at www.ICGtesting.com
LVHW040932300923
759403LV00058B/61